MEMBER OF THE HOUSE

Letters of a Congressman

MEMBER OF

Letters of a Congressman

Edited, with Additional Text by

JOHN W. BAKER
Professor of Political Science
The College of Wooster

THE HOUSE

Letters by

CONGRESSMAN CLEM MILLER

First District, California

CHARLES SCRIBNER'S SONS
NEW YORK

FOREWORD

THESE letters were conceived as illumination for interested constituents in my Congressional District who, to a large degree, shared my complete ignorance of genuine congressional activity and who lived in the history-book world of Henry Clay and Daniel Webster. I make no apologies for the letters because they are an honest effort to depict the everyday life of Congress. I make no pretensions for the letters because congressional life is more varied than can be encompassed through one window and because they were the hurried sandwich between the buzzer for the telephone and the other buzzer for my presence on the Floor. They were simply for the people of my district to share what I was learning myself. One of these was John Baker. It was he who picked up the idea of publishing the letters; he molded them into book form, assisted by his talented wife, Mary. Theirs is the credit for preparing the letters for a wider audience, and giving point and focus. Without them there would have been no book.

CLEM MILLER

PREFACE

ONCE IN a great while materials are discovered which throw new light on an old subject. These informal letters are such a find. They reflect the amazement, the amusement, the problems, and the satisfactions of a member of Congress. They were not written for publication. If publication had been planned, the material probably would have been in different form and might have lacked its fresh approach and spontaneity. The letters were not sent as general newsletters to all constituents but were written to a group of friends "who have given evidence of the greatest concern in the legislative struggle— who have done the spade work at election time." The intention was to give these people a "ringside seat" in the legislative arena.

This book is not intended to be a definitive study of Congress. It is intended to transmit the flavor of Congress as savored by an articulate congressman. The reader feels something of the shock which a person elected from a large district feels when he arrives in Washington and finds that at first he is not able to accomplish much that he really hoped to get done, let alone all that he had sincerely promised in his campaign. Evident in some of the later letters is the mellowing of three sessions of Congress. The congressman has at least become accommodated to the way Congress works and to his position in the process. If the letters had been written today, looking back on three years' experiences, many of them might well be changed rather drastically. But here they are, written while the impact of events was fresh.

The personal qualities of individual congressmen are very significant, but because this volume is more concerned with Congress collectively, many people are not identified. To avoid possible mis-understanding, unless otherwise identified, the President referred to in these letters must be remembered to be Dwight D. Eisenhower, and the Speaker of the House, the late Sam Rayburn.

The letters were written in the period of 1959 through 1961, but they are not presented in the order in which they were written. They could have been edited to reveal their time-setting, but so doing would diminish their effectiveness and freshness. I have grouped them to bring out more clearly for the reader various aspects of the legislative process. The responsibility for these groupings and for the accompanying essays is solely my own.

JOHN W. BAKER

Wooster, Ohio
April 20, 1962

CONTENTS

CHAPTER I

THE LEGISLATIVE PROCESS

A FAIRLY detailed academic description of the organization and routine of Congress and a collection of documents depicting a bill's journey through Congress are found near the end of this volume (page 141). As is the case with most textbooks, these pages describe in a somewhat mechanical way the path of a bill through Congress. A bill is introduced by a congressman, it is assigned to a committee for appropriate action, it is placed on the calendar and brought up for debate; if passed by one house, it goes through an almost identical ordeal in the other house.

This is an oversimplification of a textual oversimplification, as the following letters will show. As is usually true in matters involving many people, the procedures are not really simple. The words describing Congress which flow rather easily to the academician are often not the words which transmit to the reader the real flavor of actual happenings. They make sense sometimes, but they too often do not get the sense of Congress.

To many Americans the mention of Congress brings a vision of a great arena in which the Daniel Websters and the Patrick Henrys hammer out legislation as a result of fiery debates which sway votes and give victory to the one with the greatest logical and oratorical skill. Perhaps this was true in our formative years, when society was decidedly less complex and the powers of the national government were considered by most people to consist only of those powers specifically delegated to it by the new Constitution. But as society became more complex, so did the laws which regulated man's relationships within that society. By virtue of necessity, the demands of the populace, the Supreme Court's liberal interpretations of the Constitution, and the determination of men in the national government, the powers of that government expanded at an astonishing rate.

The population of the United States increased rapidly and so did the size of Congress, with membership in the lower house tied to population. Each new state added to the union increased the membership of the Senate by two and the House of Representatives by at least one. Shortly after the turn of the twentieth century, the House decided that it could not continue to increase in numbers as the population grew, and it voted to limit its membership to 435.

The size of the House of Representatives, the lack of real party discipline, and the multiplicity of governmental activities have severely curtailed the deliberative and legislative functions which actually take place on the Floor of Congress. Most of the action now takes place rather quietly and methodically behind closed doors and in private conversations.

Of necessity, the individual congressman must rely on the work of his colleagues in the committees. He cannot be a specialist in all areas of governmental activity—in fact, he does well to be a reasonable facsimile of a specialist in one or two areas.

Congress determines the number and variety of standing committees which will be found in each house. Each house determines the number and type of the many subcommittees set up under the parent committees.

Before the "revolution" of 1910-1911, assignment of Members to the committees and designation of the chairman were prerogatives of the Speaker of the House. Since that time, membership on the committees has been determined by the parties concerned. Status or rank on the committee, including the position of chairman, is nearly always based on the seniority of the individual committee member on that specific committee.

As simple as the mechanics of the committee system may seem, the traditional and extralegal activities and the *sub rosa* maneuverings within the committee determine finally whether or not a bill will ever become a law. Debate in the House is limited. When it is finished, the "moment of truth" theoretically arrives—the vote is taken. Actually a decisive moment occurs many times and under many circumstances in the labyrinthian path of a bill in the American legislative process.

The letters which follow in this chapter describe a portion of the legislative process as it is experienced by a *Member of the House.* A view of the operations of the standing committees is given, various "debates" are presented, and the final action of the House on a bill is pictured.

Dear Friend:

Many visitors to the Floor of the House come away disappointed. This is nothing new. Professor Woodrow Wilson reported the same reactions in 1885 when he wrote his great book—still the outstanding treatment of Congress, to my mind—*Congressional Government.*

Visitors may see a handful of Members, 50 or 60 out of 435, lounging in the great Hall of Representatives. It is half the size of a football field, and the roomy, leatherette seats are semicircled about the Speaker's dais. No one has a particular seat, but the Republicans are arranged to the left of the Speaker, the Democrats to his right. One is not supposed to read newspapers, or discuss private affairs too audibly. But frequently the buzz of conversation mounts loudly, coming readily to order under the stern, crisp orders of the Speaker.

The House Floor is a great meeting place. Since much of our time is spent in the comparative solitude of our own offices attending to district affairs, when the bells ring at noon one goes to the Floor to catch up with the latest news, the million and one small and large details of political life. One gets a line on upcoming legislation or party strategy, and so on, none of which has anything to do with what is transpiring for the record and on the record.

The congressman who is speaking is very possibly talking for the people at home. It will ALL be in the *Congressional Record;* and, by reading, other congressmen will keep abreast of whatever takes place, trivial and significant.

It is a commonplace that the work of Congress is done in committee. Here the evidence is heard, and the general approach laid down. Changes and amendments can be made on the Floor, but, generally speaking, the action there is confined to crystallizing and distilling the committee process. Debate on crucial issues is the distillate of thousands upon thousands of hours of talk that has preceded. These debates can be well attended and very lively. Or they can be deadly and irrelevant.

The House also hears Special Orders. At this time any congressman, by reserving time, can be heard for periods ranging up to an hour or two on any subject he is interested in. These speeches can be frightful or they can be fascinating. A recent speech in the House on the economy (delivered without notes) was a great contribution. (I might add that I have not seen a line about it in the press.) In this way the *Congressional Record* becomes a great catchall of significant and trivial material upon which legislation and party philosophy can be developed.

A congressman can make a fool of himself in these speeches. He has the most critical audience in the world—an audience that has spent its collective lifetime studying thin skins and stuffed shirts. Nothing gets by. Even when the speeches are poorly attended the word gets around.

To catch the attention of Congress is a neat trick in itself. Congressmen are essentially "feeling" men and women, and they respond to a feeling speech. Sincerity, conviction, speaking directly to your colleagues, count for all. The *pro forma* speech, the smart guy, the reader, count for little.

The feeling speech engenders a sense of camaraderie, even when the listener might be opposed to the ideas. And it can move the House, give it a "temper" and a "shape" it did not have a few moments earlier. And votes can be changed (as witness the vote on the Mutual Security Development Loan Fund which passed last week with a surprisingly heavy vote of 183 yeas to 59 nays after the "temper" of the House had set).

When you ask the old-timers whether you should speak on the Floor, their advice is the same—"If you feel strongly, then speak out; if you don't, let it pass."

Yet feeling speeches can fall flat. A southern congressman made a speech of "conscience" during the debate on the Deficiency Appropriation Bill. He proposed an amendment to eliminate a budget item of some $300,000 for expenses involved in sending U. S. marshals to Little Rock in 1958. He kept reminding us that this was a matter of principle and of conscience. It was poorly received. The vote was 153 nays, 43 yeas.

The House Floor is a fascinating place to be. Beneath the casual and turbid actions, an observer can glean all manner of tidbits. Who sits next to whom can furnish valuable information, or who is roaming the Floor. Where is a congressman sitting today? Who is talking to the Speaker? And so on. It is exciting and profitable for the observant, as you watch the forces at work: who is to be counted upon, how action will run, under what circumstances action can be channeled.

For example, Sam Rayburn, the Speaker, steps down from the dais, then stands on the Floor with his hawk-face beguilingly solemn; he proposes an amendment. Drily, he says as an aside, "I don't think there will be any objection to it." And in an instant, $100,000 for "Operation Outdoors"—the Outdoor Recreation Resources Review Commission—which had been completely axed in committee, was restored in full. Who had reached the Speaker? How? What prompted this unusual action? But it was done, and so simply. This is the House.

Very sincerely,

Clem Miller

Dear Friend:

While action on the Floor of the House is the "moment of truth" —when you must say "yea" or "nay"—this is only the climax of years of patient work. Most of this time is consumed in the committee to which the bill was originally assigned. Here is where Congress does its job. Here is where congressmen work on each other endless, endless hours. Here is the heart of Congress, at least of the House of Representatives.

These committee rooms can be very imposing, and the semicircle of benches quite magisterial. The Appropriations Committee Room of the new Senate Office Building must be seen to be believed. There are sheets of green marble and huge bronze fixtures. Marks of ancient Rome are immediately at hand. Other rooms are friendly and warm, with a colonial patina that is very reassuring.

Members range about the chairman according to strict seniority, Republicans on the left, Democrats on the right. Everyone has a nameplate and status is faithfully guarded.

Should the chairman of our full committee enter the hearing room during subcommittee proceedings, the sitting chairman will immediately invite him to assume the chair. It is done in a gracious, natural, and spontaneous manner that speaks respect for the authority of our senior chairman. His quiet refusal to assume the chair is equally gracious. One can see in this sort of exchange the deepest loyalties of the House to tradition and seniority. Observing these forms, it may be difficult to recall the bitter debates that have raged down through the years.

Committees are variously run, depending on the temperament of the chairman. He has the widest latitude, and he may play the Caesar role or not, as he sees fit. Most committees are run with some attention to junior members. According to seniority, they are given the privilege of questioning witnesses. This privilege is vastly appreciated when granted, resented when not. Of course, in the large committee, the pickings may be a little lean when they get down to the freshman. But, being a politician, he will extract some advantage from the most meager bones.

Congressional hearings may serve many purposes. The principal one is to build the recorded base of knowledge upon which legislation can be constructed. Even where this is the honest desire of the committee, its crabbed way must often seem strange to the untutored bystander. Many of the issues before Congress have been around for years. The chairman may be excused if he leaves holes in his investigation. Why develop a long line of inquiry when it was fully covered by Report umpty-ump of the 84th Congress?

Many times, the hearings seem to be *pro forma,* just going through the motions, with the key decisions already made. They resemble a large verbal orchestration, as a "record" is carefully shaped under the vigilant gavel of the chairman. A standard parade of witnesses files by from the national organizations—AF of L, U. S. Chamber of Commerce, National Association of Manufacturers—then a seasoning of university professors, and so on. The witnesses are carved up or blown up, or tailored to the need. Some are dismissed peremptorily, others are drawn out solicitously.

Committee members engage in pages of fulsome, politically-laden flattery. And they engage in almost unbearable cross-examination, only an eyelash from irreparable rudeness. There may be interminable irrelevance while a member chases down his own local, quirky byway to squeeze some personal advantage from a witness.

Sometimes the committee room is almost somnambulant as the hearing drifts on to arrive at its predetermined destination. Two members may be dwarfed in the large room, the lone witness below, with the court reporter puffing happily on a big cigar as he punches out the responses on his stenotype.

Other times there is excitement and novelty as, for example, listening to a tape recording of West Virginia miners out of work for two and three years—graphic testimony on the Depressed Areas Bill. Flat, soft voices, filling the room with an almost unbearable pathos. And then the blunt voice of the chairman: "That's enough of that. We get the idea."

Or there is contrast: The very large executive testifying for the National Association of Manufacturers on the same bill. A long statement, an impenetrable reading of every ponderous word. Not a single solitary sentence in the entire statement to admit that there is a depressed area problem. Accompanying him, exquisitely groomed in *haute couture,* a woman sitting behind him precisely and erectly, her mind a thousand miles away, her head turning slowly, idly, by degrees, around the room. An unforgettable scene.

Very sincerely,

Clem Miller

Dear Friend:

Hearings before congressional committees are vital and significant, but getting a hearing in the first place is quite a trick. One may have the best idea in the world, but be unable to interest the chairman of the committee sufficiently to get a hearing.

I brought with me to Washington an idea about the federal responsibility for recreation at federal reservoir sites. There is a gap in our law which should be corrected. I did some research on it through the Library of Congress. Then I took the matter up with the Interior Department. Finally, I went to see the Chairman of the Interior Committee of the House. He had only a limited time to consider the problem. He told me, "It looks like a good idea but, you know, we won't be considering legislation of this sort until after the Recreation Resources Review is finished." His remark had an air of finality.

When will the Recreation Resources Review be out? In a couple of years if we are lucky. The congressional wheel grinds slowly. There is no substantive reason to delay legislation of this sort because of the Review. However, presented with the fact that it is to be the determinant, you set about perfecting your case, hoping for a change or a day when it will be considered timely. You carry your case to interested parties—to other congressmen with similar legislation, to trade associations, and in this case to conservationists and planners. You take it to the executive branch of our government to seek a reaction.

The administrative department or agency that would be involved must file a report—setting forth its approval or disapproval—on each bill considered by Congress. Federal agencies, having been burned at the congressional stake so often, are wary. Getting an agency behind a bill is a feat in itself, even when important officials may privately favor it. If the project costs money, this Administration is almost sure to be against it. Dealing with these officials as they fence and straddle, hem, haw and pause, can be a frustrating, agonizing experience, possibly exceeded only by the frustration of the official himself.

Even if the proposal saves money, it may not get agency approval if there is offense to some philosophical concept of the Administration. It would save money to have a small, mobile maintenance crew of civil service specialists repair harbor jetties, but this appears to fly in the face of private enterprise, so no approval will be forthcoming from the dragons in the Bureau of the Budget. A bill will usually have tough sledding when it receives agency disapproval, though this is not always the case. On relatively minor matters, agency approval is vital. But as the issue increases in importance, party policy determinations loom ever larger, agency recommendations less and less.

Arresting the attention of the committee, even briefly, is a task. Two weeks ago we called the attention of the House poultry subcommittee to the frightful plight in an industry which is virtually being wiped out by high costs and low prices. There was no legislation in the hopper, there was no steam. All of a sudden, there were hearings. Congressmen living in the poultry districts of New Jersey, Ohio, Georgia, Alabama, Oklahoma, and California were getting the news from home, and a special hearing was called on an urgency basis.

Other times, you seem to have a good case, the problem is a lively one, and yet action is slow. Take the idea for reactivating the Civilian Conservation Corps. This is very much in the public eye now since several states and municipalities have taken it up on a local basis. Committee members are eager to hear it. Yet, the committee chairman seems reluctant to move. Usually, there is a reason; frequently it is not readily apparent. Then you have to go digging for it and by patient spadework allay suspicions, provide encouragement, or uncover idiosyncracies. Much of a congressman's time is taken up with this kind of sleuthing, to pry his legislation loose. Much of a congressman's effectiveness may be wrapped up in his talent for applying the leverage. This factor can be overestimated. When all is said and done, legislation seems imbued with a will of its own. At a pace which is just short of maddening, it wends its way through the process, probably to be caught fast by the end-of-session log jam.

Yet to be discussed is the importance of committee staff work. Much legislation is the product of the staff. Where a congressman must diffuse his energy over wide areas, staff members are specialists. They are bound to count heavily on technical matters. They also give shape and outline to the fuzzy legislative idea. A good chairman working with a good staff can be a joy to behold, one complementary to the other. The congressman gets an idea from home. The staff works it up and hammers it into shape. The congressman justifies the work-up to his committee, with a shrewd eye calculating his majority, stretching here, giving way there. Then it goes back to the staff for varnishing and polishing. The chairman must now stand behind his product, loyally and without misgivings—it is his responsibility. The bill is now ready for vandalism on the Floor of the House.

Very sincerely,

Clem Miller

Dear Friend:

Legislation is generally pushed out of its original shape before it arrives on the President's desk for signature. This metamorphosis along the way is the cause of much perplexity and irritation to interested citizens because the process is not clear to them.

Let us consider one place where this happens. A bill gets its first kneading at "mark-up" time in subcommittee. This is at an executive session of the subcommittee after hearings have been held. The text of the bill usually suffers insertions and additions or deletions, in a process known as "marking-up" or perfecting the bill.

The end product is the result of interaction between the committee and subcommittee chairmen, the committee staff and members of the committee. Mark-up time is also the preliminary bout between the majority (six or seven in many subcommittees) and the minority (four or five).

The committee staff has a proprietary interest in our bill. The bill we went to hearing with was probably its creature to begin with. Its details were worked out in conferences with the executive department "downtown." The staff knows every byway in the bill, has hedged against every technical problem, and tried to accommodate internal inconsistencies. Where even the most specialized congressman must turn his attention here and there whether he would or not, our bill is the life of the committee staff. It has a professional interest in the launching and the seaworthiness of the bill.

To get through mark-up time successfully, the first obstacle is the subcommittee chairman. The staff must cope with his preconceptions, prejudices, and idiosyncrasies. However it is done, the chairman must be convinced because he is the decisive influence. His lukewarmness or coolness will be immediately broadcast far and wide to make trouble in a widening pool.

While the chairman's influence is decisive, he needs support. If he has offended members of his own subcommittee, or if he disregards significant points they want to make, they will hammer in wedges that will widen as the bill proceeds along the legislative ways.

What we are seeking is maximum Majority support at mark-up

time. The hostility of the chairman is almost fatal, and division between the Majority members almost equally so. Therefore, a good staff and a good chairman will arrive at the mark-up session with their best case. This undoubtedly means a few concessions. The staff has learned what is needed in the way of concessions from the hearings.

It is often said that hearings develop the facts of the case. It may be just as properly said that hearings develop the prejudices of the sitting members, and through them the relative party stances which will be displayed later. Committee staff members follow the hearings with care. Their ears are carefully attuned, not necessarily to witnesses, but to the reactions of committee members. These revealing comments will furnish an index of opinion vital to an estimate of the concessions necessary to pass the bill.

After hearings, to be sure of some unity, the subcommittee chairman calls a meeting of Majority members to look over some possible changes in the bill. The chairman insists on informality. It is a "discussion." Nothing is to be "final." Your "ideas" are sought. One member wants a much tougher section in one part of the bill. There is chance of agreement. The staff had anticipated this with some appropriate language. Another member, not primed by a staff man, throws out an innocent suggestion which it turns out the chairman is most opposed to. The "suggestion" is permanently shelved.

Quickly the friction points are reviewed, and assent is secured for our Majority position. We are now ready for the executive session of the full subcommittee, the marking-up with a unified front. However, to achieve this we have already made several important concessions.

The Minority function at the subcommittee mark-up is to test every major segment of the bill, looking for weakness. One member leads off with a challenge to the whole bill. He has a substitute which is disposed of in a second. Then the bill is read, line by line. At the appropriate places, the Majority amendments are offered. There is some discussion. Staff members hover behind members, counselling in whispers. A vote is taken, and the clerk reads on.

At step after step the Minority amendments are offered. The attitude is offhand and perfunctory. If a glimmer of interest or a shade of response is elicited from the Majority side, the proposal is pressed. One amendment does seem reasonable. A word or two is said in its behalf. The chairman stirs about unhappily, seeing an opening wedge in Majority unity. It is disposed of, but the restlessness is noted for future exploitation by the Minority in full committee and on the Floor. Finally, the bill has been read. The disagreements—first among Democrats, then between Democrats and Republicans—have resulted in much new language, changing the shape of the bill, accommodating to our needs.

The process is repeated in full committee. Here the pressures are stronger. Weaknesses are exploited as the bill is read line by line, open to amendment at any point.

The bill is beginning to gather momentum. Committee staff strategists with an eye on the mood and temper of the House as a whole will be shaving the bill to fit. Take off $100,000,000 here to satisfy the economizers; add a Section 7(a) to please the rural congressmen. The Republicans are figuring how much they must do to hold the 65 or 70 southern Democrats they will need to win. Shave here, give there, stand fast now, and so the clerk reads on, pausing as an amendment is offered, debated up or down, then on. Finally, it is done. The bill is read. It is passed out by a predictable vote, but the bill is probably quite different than it was when it first received a number from the bill clerk two months before.

It is now ready for the Floor. The major issues are drawn clearly. One or two major points, one or two key amendments will be offered on the Floor. But the major work has been done, probably before there has been a line in the papers. The bill has been marked-up.

Very sincerely,

Clem Miller

Dear Friend:

This is mark-up time for the Public Works Bill in the Appropriations Committee. After sifting through witnesses' testimony (which takes up space the size of a New York telephone book), the committee is deciding what it will put into the bill and what it will not.

Because there is so much talk about public works and about "pork barrel," it is worth knowing something about how the whole system operates. Perhaps a better understanding of it will render a verdict that is not so harsh.

There is an elaborate procedure that a public works project must go through before it sees the light of construction. Beginning with the recommendation of the local congressman who in turn is acting on local needs, it goes through a ten-or-twelve-step approval process which includes Congress three or four times, the Corps of Engineers at many levels, the President, the Bureau of the Budget, and other interested federal and state agencies. This process ordinarily takes a long, long time. A project may never reach the construction phase. There are many excellent projects in our district authorized in 1939 or 1945 which have never received the funds to reach the final step for one reason or another.

The Corps of Engineers is the first hurdle, and perhaps the last one too. At every step their assessment of the urgency, their reports, play a vital role in the progression of the project. The Corps' evaluation is a bundle of tangibles and intangibles: "local interest," "cost-benefit ratio," "commercial use," etc.

Each year in the fall, the Bureau of the Budget, acting on the Corps' recommendations, holds flood control and harbor hearings. To hold down the budget, President Eisenhower has decreed that there shall be *no new starts*, which, when tied to a similar policy since World War II, has resulted in substantial deterioration of our public works plant. In this light, Congress has not been happy with the budget presentation which took place in January. The battle takes place in the Appropriations' Public Works Subcommittee.

Witness after witness files by—governors, senators, congressmen, county engineers, state water directors—an endless procession. Five minutes are allocated for a congressman, one hour and a half for state presentations representing millions of dollars. Our state delegation irons out its differences in advance. Our people then go in with a united front, agreed on our askings, agreed on our non-budgeted requests.

Witnesses will sell their souls for a five-minute appearance. Unlimited strategies are employed to catch the attention of committee members and the staff.

The committee, this year headed up by the tough committee chairman himself, Clarence Cannon of Missouri, then proceeds to carve out a bill. By and large the budgeted items are included fairly much as is. These may be very large items indeed, into the millions and tens of millions of dollars. It is on the nonbudgeted items that the agony begins. These items are cheap: $50,000, $35,000, $25,000. This is survey money. A survey is what the name implies, an investigation to determine the worth of the project, its feasibility and so forth. Everyone recognizes this as the first and most important hurdle. If you can get a survey, your project will probably push along to completion. The Administration realizes this, and that is why it is so anxious to hold down the surveys—total amount for *all* surveys is only two million dollars. By barring the entrance, the Administration hopes to control the whole process.

This year, the Committee has voted the exact amount of the Administration's budget proposal dollar for dollar. It comes to $1,176,677,000. They have cut down on some going projects and put in some new starts with a stiff report opposing Administration policy.

Then, it will go to the Senate which is more liberal, then to Conference with the Senate for a resolution of differences. The conference committee will horse trade back and forth, probably leaning a little to the Senate side.

This then is the Rivers and Harbors Omnibus Bill representing the will of Congress. The President will be asked to sign it.

From what I am able to observe, the Rivers and Harbors Bill is anything but pork barrel. In point of fact, from our experience in the First District, it is quite inadequate. This problem of national needs vs. budget-balancing vs. inflation is perhaps the greatest three-ringed argument in the U. S. today.

Very sincerely,

Clem Miller

Dear Friend:

This letter will try to give you the flavor of the House debate on civil rights—through excerpts from the *Congressional Record*.[1]

A Democrat from New York led off the debate: "Mr. Chairman, I think of the whole world, with little children yet to be born. They will enter into life with sweet and innocent ignorance—that their differences in color will place upon them burdens too heavy for those little shoulders to carry—and early in childhood they will meet with a prickling of the heart and spirit, the ugliness of discrimination.

"Does it have to be? No. We can—if only we wish it—erase that ugliness. The world is wide enough to embrace differences in religion and in color. Indeed, it is these very differences that make for the dynamics and vitality of living. . . .

"All we ask is recognition of difference. To those who prate of their better or noble blood, I say, go to the market place and see what your blood will buy. To those gentlemen who boast of their sacred way of life and their living under their family tree, I say, living under the shadow of a family tree means living without sunlight—the sunlight of reason and tolerance.

"Fundamentally, we are here to determine whether the Constitution of the United States is a vital, living document for some and a dead letter for others . . . we stand here on the bedrock of the Constitution of the United States, to preserve its integrity and to give it the springs to catapult it into action. Without appropriate enforcement provisions, the Constitution remains a group of paragraphs insulated from the life of the people like some archaic document in a glass caged museum, a closet drama to be read but not played.

"We are concerned here with the constitutionally guaranteed rights which deny to both Federal and State government the au-

[1] These excerpts from the *Congressional Record* beginning here and ending on page 26 did not follow each other directly but occurred in this order. The debates actually took place over a period extending from March 10 through March 23, 1960, and were the main order of business each day that the House was in session.

The paragraphing of the *Congressional Record* has not always been followed.

thority to withhold from the people the equal protection of the laws or to discriminate against some of the people because of race or color."

A Democrat from Kentucky: "Far less than this provoked the Civil War back in 1861. . . . Certainly I know that I am more interested in the solution of racial differences, if any there may be, than a lot of these so-called professional "do-gooders" running around the country, who are really no more concerned about the colored man's problems than Sally Rand is in doing her fan dance in a tin kimono. And when there is no more civil rights ballyhoo left to exploit, this group of professional sadhearts will be about as useful as the last note played in the 1901 fiddlers' contest. . . .

"There is one small basic thing that the leaders of the NAACP and the CORE have either forgotten or unfortunately have never been taught—that real ladies and gentlemen with good breeding, first, never ask or seek an invitation; second, do not go where they are not invited; third, nor do they remain where they are not wanted. These lunch counter students are only hurting their cause. Their leadership is as shaky as the guest bookstand in an undertaker's parlor and is about as dependable as a blown fuse in a lightning bug's tail light. You cannot legislate morals any more than you can force some people to accept the friendship of others. The good Lord gave me my relatives but I reserve the right to fully select my own friends and associates. And when the time comes that I cannot, we have had it in the United States. . . .

". . . in 1861, there were those who were hotheaded, impatient, tactless, arrogant, who literally tried to cram thorny issues down the delicate throats of tolerant people. And what was the result? . . . Destruction, grief, misery, and poverty followed this unnecessary war. You can crowd people just so far. The same is true today. Unfortunately, the deep wounds and broad scars that were inflicted between 1861 and 1865 have not fully healed and yet there are those today very much like those of yesteryear, who, if they had their way, would literally push this Nation into another civil conflict and I am afraid we are about to have one. . . ."

A Democrat from California: "We have had many people come to the shores of the United States in more recent times. My own parents were among these. They suffered a measure of discrimination because they did not speak well, or their skin was slightly darker, or their ways were strange but they came out of it. They obtained positions of great recognition and were permitted to move freely in society and they lived in neighborhoods unmolested. I am informed that the Vice-President of the United States lives in a house that bears a covenant which says it shall not be sold to Syrians—that is what we Lebanese were called before 1943—Negroes, Orientals, and so on. We see how recently this discrimination was being practiced on an even wider scale. Yet, I stand here in the Congress of the United States. . . . Why were these people able to rise and the Negroes were not? The answer is simple. They were not denied access to the schools. They were not excluded from the business community; they were not relegated to the most menial tasks and denied adequate opportunity to improve themselves. They were not intimidated by force and violence and threats. In short they were not segregated nor disenfranchised."

A Democrat from Alabama: ". . . if I could be so bold as to offer to the Members of this House one suggestion, it would be this: Let us take first things first. Let us recognize the need for national unity in this country against our foreign enemies and, once we have solved the problems which we face overseas, then we can go about doing what many people seem to think amounts to setting our own house in order."

A Republican from New York: "No government with any claim to legitimacy can give—or take away—a person's civil rights. Civil rights are not created by governments. They are only recognized, and formulated into legal and constitutional expressions, and protected by civil authority—or, as the case may be, denied and abused by public authority. Civil rights, I believe, are essential corollaries of human rights; the expression in our written law of the unwritten basis of Western civilization—that every human person is a sacred reality and as such is entitled to the opportunity of fulfilling those great human potentialities with which God has endowed every man."

A Democrat from Tennessee: "Let me say . . . that the gentleman from California is totally ignorant of the way of life enjoyed by the people in the South; he is wholly unacquainted with the public school systems of the several States of the South, and I dare say he is uninformed about anything that applies to the culture and the way of life of a great people."

A Democrat from Mississippi: ". . . I do not think this is a day of which we . . . can be proud. There are those who will of course contend that they are looking after the so-called civil rights of some of our citizens. They will bemoan the alleged misfortunes and mistreatments of these citizens, demand passage of a law, and then quietly return to their own segregated way of living. Their first interest, in fact their genuine interest, is not in the enactment of a new civil rights law. Their first interest is their own political position, their re-election come next November, or possibly their election to an even higher office than that which they now hold. Strong pressures are being brought to bear. In response to these pressures this subject is now before the Congress and that is the only reason it is here."

A Democrat from Georgia: "That [Civil Rights] Commission made seriously the recommendation that you amend your Constitution and let a 23rd amendment provide that just any old person who can satisfy the State's age requirements and residence requirements and is not in jail shall be a legal voter. Do you doubt that? That is what that says. If you are an idiot or a lunatic or just a natural-born fool, and you are not in jail, you can vote. What can you do with that kind of stuff? You had better get rid of that Civil Rights Commission, because the administration that appointed them has repudiated every recommendation they made, and I challenge anybody to dispute it. They made several recommendations and every one has been discarded, operating on the idea that it did not reflect credit upon a person 10 years of age. So much for that Commission. . . . In Georgia we do have a literacy test and we have the questions. If he flunks them one time, the NAACP says "You come down to the

St. Mary's, Methodist, Episcopal, or Baptist Church on Sunday," and they teach him for weeks and weeks and weeks until he can answer all those questions like you would teach a parrot."

A Democrat from California: "We are helping to shape this story of freedom as we deliberate on the matter before us. We have but three choices—to add another worthy chapter to the story of human progress, or to leave the chapter unwritten to be taken care of another day, or possibly to accept a halfway measure on the theory that half a loaf is better than none. I do not believe the great majority of American people will be satisfied with anything less than the first choice. We shall stagnate as a democracy, we shall dull our image before the world, we shall obviate our constitutional and moral precepts if we fail to resolve the civil rights issue of our day."

A Democrat from Arkansas: "The one prevailing thought of the advocates of civil rights legislation has continually been to give some congressional status or standing to that ill-considered opinion of the Supreme Court which knocked down the traditional and constitutionally proper pattern of separate but equal in the public schools as determined by the respective States. . . . Before that tragic unconstitutional decision of the Supreme Court . . . there was relative tranquility between the white and Negro races of our Nation. This applied not only to the South, but to the North, East, and West, where people live together with respect and consideration of the rights of others. But since the day of that totally unconstitutional decision, much of our tranquility has been destroyed. . . . We need to examine the Constitution through the eyes of our Founding Fathers; we must repudiate the pragmatic prating and preaching of alien ideologies."

A Democrat from Connecticut: ". . . several months ago, we were debating the rights of union members to vote. I recall that many of my friends in this Chamber vociferously reminded us that the basic voting rights of even such a small minority of our citizenry must be strongly defended by proper legislation. It saddens me to note how still, how muffled these once strong voices in behalf of basic human rights have become."

A Democrat from Mississippi: "People of the South, standing together, make up the most potent minority in these United States. Continue this campaign of vilification against the integrity and the institutions of our people and you will see a political uprising in the South that will challenge the position of both major political parties. The South today has such strength in the electoral college that no Democratic candidate can be elected President of the United States without our support. You are driving us out of the party of our fathers."

Another Democrat from Mississippi: "Let us see what it is possible for the people of the South to do. If involved here are the efforts of these two major parties to elect a President and control the Congress . . . first we should look to the Constitution to see how a President is elected. . . . it is entirely up to the State as to how it shall select electors and as to whether they shall pledge them to the nominees of either party or shall leave them to their independent judgment.

"Now, if the Southern States should follow that course, the independent electors might vote for the Democratic nominee. They might vote for the Republican nominee; and yes, it is true that they might vote for a third candidate. As we all can recognize, under such a procedure if division was close enough between the Democrats and Republicans they could throw the election into the House of Representatives.

"Now we turn to the election of the Speaker of the House of Representatives and the organization of that body, and we find that the House of Representatives shall choose their Speaker and other officers. In 1809 it was held that the Speaker should be elected by a majority of those present, and in 1879 that it might be elected by a majority of those present of a quorum; and a majority of all the Members was not required. . . . In Jefferson's *Manual* and reading in the Constitution we see that a Speaker may be removed by the will of the House, and a Speaker pro tempore appointed. The meaning of this . . . is that a majority of the House of Representatives can change Speakers from time to time under the rules, if it so desires.

"Thus, after we note these provisions we see that there are several courses the people of the Southern States could take. First, the South could in their respective states set up a third party with respective nominees for President and Vice-President. Here, frankly, the competition for who rides the white horse might prevent such a move getting enough support to count. Another approach . . . would be to select independent electors to cast their votes in the electoral college as best they could. Third, southern Members of Congress could unite and make it necessary for a coalition to organize the Congress. Ninety-three Members voted against the rule on the measure before us. It is apparent that such 93 could have changed control of the House when this Congress was organized.

"I point out these possibilities here today because you need to know what you are forcing the people of a large section of our country to consider. . . . We all know that many southerners now in Congress, because of various reasons, key position, the acclaim they receive, and other things, would not like to go along'with this at the moment; but I say to you that the people back in our respective districts and our respective States are after all in the final analysis going to govern. I say to you that under the usual division between the major parties here, if one-third of all the southerners in the Congress were to unite along either of these lines it would make it necessary for those who did not, to run 'on the other side.' Few would take that course."

A Democrat from South Carolina: "We are witnessing the gambling for the raiment of the crucified body of the South. These fellows on my left and on my right have decided they have the votes. What do they care about the Constitution? They have the votes. It is a cheap and hypocritical bid for the votes to the left and for the Negro votes of the vastly populated areas on the East, the Far West, and the Midnorthwest. . . ."

A Democrat from Georgia: "I am tired of this helpless Negro stuff I hear so much talk about. They got after me one day about the way I pronounced that word. I have never had any trouble with a nigger in my life, but oh, my God, that "neegro," I have had plenty with him. . . ."

A Democrat from Florida: "Congress now is legislating under duress. Demonstrations which are a tribute only to behind the scenes Communist organizing, and which frequently are coupled with violence, shame our land. The Congress should suspend all consideration of this measure until these demonstrations end. It should never be reported to the world that the forces of democracy work in this manner, or that Congress can be coerced and intimidated by fear of reprisal at the polls."

Very sincerely,

Clem Miller

Dear Friend:

Every time we want to catch our breath with some trivia, there are major events to retail in these letters. I am in the Old Office Building, a huge square with a hollow center, wide corridors, high ceilings. Old-fashioned railroad car carpeting. High-backed leather chairs. If you take away the electric typewriters, you move right into the world of William Howard Taft. There is a New Office Building —I don't care for it. Low ceilings, panelled walls, smacking of a 1925 corporation lawyer. In either place, the congressman feels crowded. Whether he is or not, that is another matter. He has an office to himself where he can immure himself if he wishes. Wisely, few try it. In our other room, we have four secretaries. We sort through the mail, and the day's clatter begins. There is checking with federal agencies; there are claims, wrongs, suggestions, requests, threats, promises; everything is filtered and answered as completely as possible, as straightforwardly as possible and as quickly as possible.

An assistant works patiently on legislative matters, bills we are interested in, appropriations, and tries to keep track of what is going on in Congress and at home. This is a huge, never-ending, and frustrating job because a million things are happening every day.

This last week was the week of the four-year Draft Extension. It sailed through the House. Continuation of the draft presented some sticky problems, but no one had any acceptable alternative. The matter was brought up very swiftly and went through the Armed Services Committee with a minimum of hearing. Whether this haste was to foreclose on opponents, I cannot say, but it was very fast.

A kind of caucus was held a day before the debate. The opposition to the four-year extension centered around a freshman congressman who had made much of the issue in his campaign. His proposal was the mildest: Lower the draft to two years while remedies are found for an ailing system. The caucus made it apparent that there would be no organized defense of the amendment he proposed. There were too many different voices, and no one to coordinate them and discipline the presentation. Those who wanted a complete end to the draft were going to use this occasion to present their case before the bar of public opinion. Those who espoused the two-year extension could not present a case clear-cut enough to win over the nonfreshman group. But the caucus really foundered on the imperturbable manner and potent influence of a senior congressman from the committee who showed up to tell the caucus why the Armed Services Committee had done what it had.

Here is where leadership makes itself felt. With good humor, patience, and considerable forbearance, this congressman cut the support for the amendment in two. No one could challenge the congressman's devotion to forward-looking programs. Several men said, "If people like —— of Illinois are going along with the Leadership, we have no case." He left the meeting. The amendment was finished before it was proposed on the Floor.

Next day, the Chairman of the Armed Services Committee presented the bill. Graciously he offered the opposing congressman all kinds of time. (Debate is limited, and minutes are treasured.) The congressman spoke eloquently. The hostility stiffened. The chairman put his arm around the opposition leader.

The only moment of concern came when a congressman from Connecticut spoke to the issue—two years to study alternatives—you could see the party whips stirring through the Chamber looking for signs of defection.

Then the debate went off on a tangent. Each of the small band of spokesmen for limiting the draft went his own way. For the committee, the debate concluded with a most sincere and liberal congressman hinting, in a voice choked with emotion, that it would be unpatriotic to vote against the four-year extension. Coming from this gentleman, it was very effective.

The vote came on the amendment—a voice vote, the nays had it, and a stand-up (division) vote was not even asked for.

What had happened? First, there was no opposition to the four-year extension coming from *within* the originating Committee of Armed Services, and this consigned the overturning effort to failure from the start. Next, the chairman cut away other possible support by appointing a subcommittee to study the matter. Thirdly, there were no older Members of the Congress who would join the freshmen in opposition. To a man they felt that there was too much risk of debate going sour without any rewards which would make such risk worthwhile. They did not want to be labelled as associating with "trouble-makers" and "crackpots" unless some objective could be achieved. For example, one of these congressmen had prepared some remarks. When he saw how the debate was going, he inserted his speech in the *Record* without reading it.

Debate is a dangerous thing. It can take the good down with the bad. Debate on the four-year extension was querulous, repetitive, rather flat, and largely irrelevant. Old hands had felt this might result, hence they avoided the arena.

Very sincerely,

Clem Miller

Dear Friend:

The debate over the Mutual Security Bill (foreign aid) took four days. A lot of words were put in the *Record* but it was my own view that everyone's mind was made up before the gavel sounded for the opening.

"Foreign Aid" is heard from every day in Congress, and is generally rung in to describe every United States fiscal shortcoming. It is the most worked over $3.6 billion in the federal budget. One could observe the build-up of hostility to it from the opening of Congress. Important blocs of votes were eroding away. This seemed particularly true in the South (eight votes were lost between 1958 and 1959). But a member, from the Midwest, said, "I campaigned against it; I guess I'll have to vote against it, no matter what."

The Foreign Affairs Committee had worked hard on the bill. In times past a Midwest Republican with a very sharp tongue had his own way in the committee. This time, however, an east coast Democrat with experience in the Far East became the rallying point for debate.

His general premise was, "Sure, there is waste. Certainly, it is inefficient, but the future of world peace depends on holding our allies, and particularly countries like Turkey and India. Sure, the Mutual Security framework is inadequate, and the Executive has blundered, but this is not the year to make drastic changes. It can't be done."

The problem is how to reconcile profound disquietude with the way things are going, with the overriding necessity of continuing the program.

The committee handled this very neatly. The bill provided a total of $3.64 billion. To appease the economizers this total represented $267 million less than the President asked for. But it was $214 million *more* than Congress appropriated last year. To appeal to the liberals, the cuts in the President's proposal came almost entirely from military support ($245 million) while there were actual additions ($100 million) on the economic side.

The committee report stood the shock of congressional Floor debate very well. The "experts," the congressmen with access to "secret" reports, all inveighed against military cuts. It was a test of instinct vs. the expert. The "experts" used everything—insults, superciliousness, patronization, sarcasm. The Defense Department was quoted and requoted backward and forward heralding a disaster. However, the growing disenchantment with the very premises upon which our military support to many foreign countries rests simply would not down.

In fact, on the key amendment vote of the bill, the antimilitary support forces came within two votes of cutting the military another $165 million. The vote on this crucial amendment was 101 to 103.

The leaders in the Foreign Affairs Committee sought to draw a fine line between the possible and the ideal. In addition to the mood of Congress, which they felt put a ceiling on the possibilities, the Mutual Security Bill (actually an *amendment* to the Act passed in 1954) posed considerable problems in itself. It is a poor instrument of policy. One of the committee leaders tried to handle this diplomatically by inserting some additional language into the Act's "Statement of Policy." The language contains phrases such as "the survival of the U. S. depends on broader freedom everywhere," and that the U. S. has an "abiding interest" in assisting other nations to secure freedom. This was aimed at diverting the military emphasis of the program to broader goals. A Republican from Michigan sought to eliminate the word "abiding" from this inoffensive and well-stated preamble. It is a significant measure of the pettiness of this debate that his amendment succeeded 64 to 54.

It is of significance here because it points up the difficulties of enacting legislation. Many congressmen know that we need a newly drafted Mutual Security Act. Since this is impossible to get, they seek by amending the statement of intent to open the way for the Executive to make such changes without legislative action. However, they do not dare go far, because the narrow motives that rule many congressmen promptly come into play. Hence, such things as the amendment mentioned above. This group is saying, "We know what you are up to, and we probably can't stop that, but we will show you what we mean by taking out a word—we might have an 'interest' in other nations but it shall not be an 'abiding' one."

Finally, Mutual Security for 1959 passed with a vote of 271 to 142. Last year it was 259 to 134. The figures seem about the same, but actually Mutual Security lost ground. Since many isolationists had retired last year and their places were filled by more internationally oriented Democrats, it meant a rising old-timer vote against "foreign aid."

Very sincerely,

Clem Miller

Dear Friend:

It is only rarely, it seems to me, that congressional debate shows real technical excellence. The real footwork on legislation is done in committee, or elsewhere. Actual debate usually proceeds lamely, hampered by the limitations on time imposed by our very size.

The ability to persuade by argument is generally reserved for borderline cases. This occurs on bills involving detailed facts and figures. I think congressmen really assembled to hear a congressman from Texas give us the facts about the Veterans Pension Bill this year. I think there was quite a bit of listening on the Mutual Company Insurance Tax Bill, weighing the pros and cons.

Mostly, even when you are following the course of debate fairly closely, you find that you are searching for the corroboration of attitudes that have already become somewhat fixed.

That is why the appearance of two debaters who apparently win votes on the Floor, in the time allotted, is quite a rarity. Such a moment was on June 23 when a congressman from Alabama pulled the Housing Bill fat out of the fire where another talented congressman, from Texas, had placed it.

The Texan only had five minutes to do his work. This was all the time he was given. The bill had been passed previously and was back on the House Floor as a compromise measure between the House and Senate. The whole debate took only an hour. But the key to the debate was the five minutes apiece that the Texas congressman and his colleague from Alabama took.

Both gentlemen use the southern style which means skill with the voice itself, but both employ subtleties that take the edge off the florid phrases of other practitioners. The voices of both are round and full, and come over the "mike" with true volume. But it is volume controlled.

The Texan starts out very softly. He takes a considerable part of his five minutes to tell us how fine a man the gentleman from Alabama is, what a fine job the conference committee has done. He bathes the Chamber with friendly feeling. A smile is playing over his lips and he keeps rising on his toes and hunching into the mike to include us all in this friendly glow.

He speaks from the mike located among his fellow congressmen. He always does. Not from the mike in the well of the House. This gives everyone the idea that he is one of us, with us, expressing our hopes. He is not lecturing or telling, he is projecting on our behalf.

He is speaking his own mind, in his humble judgment, and he is with us because he voted with us, and he is going to vote to override the President's veto, and, to please the liberals, he thinks too much has been made about costs, etc. It is really good. He has appealed to everyone on *behalf* of everyone.

But then the hooker slams in. The bill uses the backdoor to the Treasury! The smile disappears. The voice thunders. The bushy eyebrows become thoroughly menacing. The hands which had been conducting an orchestra become the fists of a heavyweight boxer. He sways back as he hits from the floor. He says, "The important thing in this bill was the thing which was taken out. I hope that is clear." These simple words are full of threat and menace.

And in less than a second, the artist changes pace, loading sarcasm on Congressman ——, shame for knuckling under to the Senate; and with it he appeals to our pride. Are we not equal and coordinate with the Senate? Are we going to let them browbeat us?—and at this point he comes down hard, putting backbone into us, "Let us not duck out of that."

Now that our courage is screwed up, he is going to show us how we do it. Dancing up and down on his toes, again hands leading an orchestra, shifting his glasses back and forth on top of his head or over his eyes, keeping our attention by manipulation, he is going to lead us along the way. It is a "complicated parliamentary procedure, and there is no need of going into that"—he will take care of it. All we have to do is vote down the report, and send the committee back to the Senate. Part of his skill is in wrapping up contrary emotions into single packages. For example, the conferees are going to be reasonable, they are going to give, but they are going to stick to principle. This conflict, when tied together by such a master, sounds very convincing. Finally, he closes. Opening his arms to the widest extent, standing erect like a marshal: "Mr. Speaker, let us vote down this bill and send these able men back—and they are good, and they are fine, and they are grand—and tell them to stand hitched. . . ." He has done his job.

Very sincerely,

Clem Miller

Dear Friend:

When the congressman from Texas concluded his speech on the Housing Bill, there was a definite feeling through the Chamber that he had hit hard. Everyone had listened, and that was a rarity in itself. There was a stirring and rustling in the seats. A switch of twenty-five votes could be disaster for the bill. Another congressman, former county district attorney and state senator, Chairman of the Housing Committee, was responsible for the countermoves. He has a gray, placid, serious face. When he is chatting with someone the face is extremely mobile and lights up in every corner; while he speaks, his pleasant smile comes across. During this effective speech, he remained slouched inert in his seat, apparently inattentive. It seemed he was never going to make his move.

Finally, he heaved to his feet as though it required a mighty effort. The gentleman from Alabama speaks from the well of the House. He pauses for a moment to get attention. Waiting is hard to do in the House. Many congressmen could wait forever and the hubbub would only increase. He uses the lean-back style rather than the hunch-forward. He leans back like a great pitcher. When he throws, he does so with his guileless friendly face thrusting out his chin to everyone in the room. The grayness is all gone. Everyone is caught up in his words.

His voice is rich and deep and droll. "I am a little bit amazed," he starts out, lingering over his amazement; and from the way he says it, you know that it is only a "little" bit. He is amazed that the Texan's cohorts are complaining about $500 million for urban renewal, when the bill with their amendment called for a billion— twice as much. Who are the spenders now?

Then he stops. He peers around the room, puts his glasses on, and turns squarely to the Republican side of the Chamber. "I would like to see the hands raised of those who would like to vote for a billion dollars of urban renewal the first year." Absolute silence. Stunned silence.

Wagging his head for the response, he waits and waits and waits in the pin-drop quiet of the Chamber. Then, just when it seems like some are recovering from the shock, and an arm is reaching for the Floor mike, he rushes on to his climax. "I am willing to yield the floor to *anybody* who can show . . . that the bill as amended did not have one billion dollars the first year for urban renewal." A master stroke, if he can hold it. There is an answer, an easy one. The speaker waits, inert, draping himself over the lectern carelessly. Two Republicans say something. It's not to the point at all. One says, "It's hard to understand—" and the chairman cuts in, "It's not hard to understand." The opposition gets the range, he starts to get the point. The chairman is in full control, telling his opponent expansively and indulgently, "Of course it does, there is no way around it."

And with this he wheels about ceremoniously from the Republican to the Democratic side. He twits the economizers a little, surprised they want a billion dollars the first year instead of $500 million. He is sure his friend from Texas did not know that. He is willing to yield to his friend if he is wrong. The gentleman from Texas was in the back of the Chamber, he was not coming forward, so the chairman digs in a little deeper. "The facts are, my friends, that when you start messing with a complex bill of this kind, you are in danger of either ruining the legislation or getting yourself in trouble." The Texan started coming down the aisle. He was flushed and thunderous. Everyone was watching for signs and portents. He reaches the mike. It is apparent that he is fencing for a delay to collect himself. He shifts uncertainly from one mike to another, almost loses his balance. "Am I right?" the chairman snaps out.

"I think you are right, Mr. Chairman, but. . . ." He was finished. He could have talked for an hour. He was through. The lost votes were regained. He drifts on, arriving at the conclusion that his friend from Alabama is "making a mountain out of a molehill."

The Alabaman, who had already won, could do it now with a flourish—"A billion dollars is considerable of a molehill."

He returned to his seat. "That was close," he said ruefully. "—— was mad, but he promised me he wasn't going into that amendment."

It takes a bold man to gamble the way the chairman did. At any one of three or four places in this short exchange, the result could have gone the other way. It did not because he was the expert in housing, and the others were not. He had the initiative, they did not. He was willing to press the point, the others did not dare.

This was a skillful, bold offensive. The billion dollar argument he used was actually irrelevant to the proposed amendment. He could not make a dent in the amendment with the Texan's supporters. The same men, however, were the economizers, so he appealed to them directly. This took quick thinking. The billion dollar argument had serious flaws in it. It took boldness to use it, good generalship to carry it through.

And boldest of all, in this rapacious Chamber, were the stunning offers to yield the floor, to invite rebuttal, instead of seeking to head it off.

This was a brilliant exercise of skill. It signifies much more than that. It means you must know your subject. The chairman did, his opposition did not. If it had, the Housing Bill could have been lost then and there.

Very sincerely,

Clem Miller

Dear Friend:

There are all sorts of ways to get things done in Congress. The best way is to live long enough to get to be a committee chairman, and resilient enough to be a good one. Chairmen complain to me that they are frustrated too, but this is really beside the point. If things can be done, they can do them; we are very sure of that.

However, there are other ways, and one of the most effective persons is a congressman from Florida. I first met him at a congressional children's party where he was joyously and enthusiastically larruping up the crowd with imitations of frogs, pigs, and other noisy animals.

I soon learned that this is the man's trademark—the joyful and enthusiastic acceptance of life. His brief appearances on the House Floor are always heralded with high good humor. The somber aspect of the Chamber takes on a lighter hue. Members stream in from the cloakroom. "——is on," is the word. "Did you hear what he told them?"

After one of his speeches, everyone feels better and usually the Member from Florida feels the best of all. This congressman rarely speaks without a purpose, larded as it is with friendliness and cheer.

He has an angular face with a turned up chin, giving it a puckish cast. His voice is melodious enough, but when he calls out, he can be heard through a six-inch mahogany door. As he talks he leans into his audience (most of our good talkers are leaners) and cocks his head to one side like a mocking bird.

And this man can charm the birds out of the trees. Partisan lines soften, and political gunboats cease cannonading, and the hard-bitten appropriations chairmen vie with one another for the nicest things to say.

To tackle the Appropriations Committee on the Floor of the House is a major decision, frequently the most important decision a Member will make that term of Congress. Here is the choice. If he is silent, perhaps the Senate will restore the item to the bill. If he speaks up and is beaten, he will *never* get it back. And the chances of winning are better than five hundred to one against. These odds mean silence to most congressmen, but not to the Florida representative.

First, he sets the stage in the hearing on the Rule by telling everyone what he is going to do.

"Mr. Chairman, at the appropriate time, I intend very humbly and very prayerfully to offer an amendment. I hope the gentleman from Texas, my distinguished, intellectual leader and my athletic leader, will help me a little bit with it and if he would I would bestow upon him the highest accolade of all and call him my spiritual leader, if he will help me to correct an injustice that I know he does not want to be meted out upon the gentleman from Florida. . . . I know that this Committee will not be unfair to the gentleman from Florida and deny him his laboratory when some of you have received so much."

Everyone is put in a receptive mood by being told with what fear and trepidation he approaches the task. Everyone trembles before the Appropriations Committee so that his well-planned fright is shared by all, and vastly appreciated. He casts an apprehensive eye at the Committee Chairman.

He spins out his dilemma. He knows he can get this entomological laboratory if he will wait till January, 1961, but for this, that, and the other reason he wants to get started in 1960. We all understand these dilemmas. We share the explicit and implicit direction of his remarks; our empathy adds savor to the whole performance.

Then he goes to work on the main redoubts. He offers an amendment. He cocks his head. The Committee Chairman, on his feet in an instant, says, "Mr. Chairman, I reserve a point of order." Ruefully, but with the utmost grace, the Florida congressman backs away: "I ask unanimous consent to withdraw the amendment and offer another one." No one objects.

"Mr. Chairman, I appreciate the courtesy of my beloved chairman." When this congressman says "beloved" the word has substance and meaning. He really likes people; and usually, in politics, among professionals, this is hard to get across.

There follows a lightning-quick description of what the amendment would do. He ripples over it like a dancer. No waste motion, no bogging down in boring detail. Enough, but not too much. Thus he disarms the opposition with his nimble tracery.

"I want to apologize to many of my friends because I told you this amendment would not cost you any more money. If my first amendment had been in order it would not have. Please forgive that error. I would like you to vote against me if you think I have misled you."

There follows a neat fencing match with the Floridian tripping a light step between the ranking Republican and the Committee Chairman, the master, who realizes he has a past master on his hands. He begs his friend from Florida to hold off until January, to which the latter responds:

"Sir, I am put in an embarrassing situation. Mr. Chairman, may I say I would be grateful if I could have action now; and if I am not successful I know my dear friend would not hold it against me for making this attempt. Then if I am not successful in this attempt, I can come back in January."

His five minutes expire, but the delighted House, by unanimous consent, permits him to proceed for three more minutes. In the general levity which followed, I admitted we have bugs in my district and we want them eradicated. He beamed his broadest and repeated with comical inflection: "Bugs in California? I thank the gentleman. . . ." The House roared in enjoyment.

A Member from Ohio rose to suggest that we delete some funds for a monument and use it to get rid of insects.

Another congressman from Iowa suggested we not only want to get rid of bugs but we want to return this wonderful person to Congress next year.

Our Florida colleague beamed and bobbed at the Speaker's lectern, telling us he would be overjoyed to yield to Members who would say such nice things about his laboratory.

The Committee Chairman threw up his hands and sat down. The amendment was agreed to by voice vote.

Everyone was happy.

Very sincerely,

Clem Miller

Dear Friend:

When the House does finally act, it does so with speed. The final arrival of a bill on the Floor is usually the result of agonizing months and years of work and maneuvers. But, once before the House, it goes up or down in short order.

However, when legislation comes to the Floor outside the ordinary channels, the picture changes. Matters of form, ordinarily taking seconds, may take hours. This is what occurs when "Calendar Wednesday" is employed. Calendar Wednesday was originally devised in 1909 to circumvent the iron rule of the Speaker. In recent years, it has been attempted only once. It is bitterly opposed by the traditionalists because it proceeds outside the regular order of things.

According to the rules, on Wednesday each committee, in alphabetical rotation, is permitted to bring up one bill without going through the Rules Committee. Some weeks ago, after a year of struggling with the Rules Committee for a Rule on the Area Redevelopment Bill, our committee decided to try the unusual Calendar Wednesday procedure. Thereupon, the Majority Leader was notified that the usual procedure of dispensing with Calendar Wednesday by unanimous consent would be objected to.

This threw the machinery into action. The Speaker ordered the call of the committees under Calendar Wednesday procedure.

An opponent of our bill made a point of order that a quorum was not present, and a count revealed this to be the case. Three roll calls were then necessary to dispose of this delaying tactic. Each roll call takes about a half hour.

Next, the *Daily Journal* of the events of the preceding day was read in full, instead of being dispensed with in the ordinary manner. Halfway through, the leader of the obstructionists made another point of order that a quorum was not present. There was not, and again it took four roll calls.

As the formality of reading the *Journal* was being resumed, a third point of order was raised on absence of a quorum. Most southerners and Republicans left the Chamber so that a quorum was almost impossible to find. Again, three roll calls were needed to get back on the legislative track.

At 4:30 P.M. the House had been in session more than four hours, and the legislation itself had yet to be reached. At this point the Majority Leader asked for unanimous consent to dispense with further reading of the *Journal,* and there was no objection. The opposition had relented. Finally our committee chairman was able to call up the bill for consideration. At this point the Minority Leader demanded a roll call vote on whether the bill should come before the House. He lost, 221 to 171, but the entire bill had to be read, 36 pages of it.

The Republicans offered a substitute and this had to be read almost in its entirety. Then a series of substitutes and amendments were offered, most of which were considered as read because there was no objection to considering them.

Through the two hours of actual debate few of the many dilatory tactics that might have been employed were brought into play. Still, it was 9:30 P.M. before voting on final passage of the bill began. For two hours of debate the House had been in session continuously for ten hours.

The Area Redevelopment Bill passed—202 to 184. But defenders of the "regular order" made sure the lesson was well impressed on us that Calendar Wednesday is not a royal road to congressional objectives.

Very sincerely,

Clem Miller

Dear Friend:

I am going to use the next two newsletters to describe the machinery which propels legislation through the House. These letters should be helpful in explaining actions of the House which otherwise, in news accounts, may appear perverse and incomprehensible.

Let us begin with a bill, say, in the Interior Committee. It has been the subject of hearings in a subcommittee; then it was considered and reported out favorably in executive session of the full committee. The Speaker of the House now places it on the Union Calendar, and it is referred to the Rules Committee for a hearing. All bills do not wind up in the Rules Committee, but our bill, which is somewhat controversial and involves money, certainly will be channeled there.

We should note the fact that this authority to refer bills, to sidetrack them or pigeonhole them through the various calendar devices, is one of the principal power levers of the Speaker. Particularly for lesser legislation (which may be the lifeblood of individual congressmen) the chasm between the standing committee and the House Floor is bridged with the unchallenged power of the Speaker. He has many combinations of courses available to him through this complex labyrinth. This power is not infinite by any means. The opposition is alert. The right to object is available at every hand, and is used promptly. It takes skill, aided by access to the inside track, to use the various means at a time and place when the objectors aren't on hand. The most widely known example of that this year was the Un-American Activities Committee appropriation which came to the Floor like a thunderclap as a privileged matter and was over and done within thirty seconds, while the potential objectors were miles away.

To return now to our bill from Interior before the Rules Committee. The Rules Committee takes testimony. Seated around an oval green baize table, with no reporter present, the questioning is very informal. Witnesses are ordinarily congressmen, most frequently the principal opponents and proponents. Much of the discussion on important bills has been repeated year after year. The hearings I have attended have been extremely rancorous, with argument largely in clichés and stereotypes, expressive of attitudes rather than of much effort at fact-finding. The Rules Committee has on its membership the most conservative Members of Congress. Its chairman readily admits to his conservatism and says freely that he does not interpret his function as one to preside over the demise of the old order.

The purpose of this hearing is to decide whether a "Rule" will be granted. A Rule is in the form of a resolution, and it fixes the terms and conditions of debate in the House. Without a Rule, it is very difficult, indeed, to bring a bill to the House Floor. One means, Calendar Wednesday, we have described in a previous letter.

The Rule fixes the time limit for debate. It limits the number of amendments which may be offered (or grants open amendment). With its power to grant or withhold a Rule, the Rules Committee can exert great force on the kind of bill which will be debated. The School Support Bill, for example, was rewritten in the Education Committee, not in terms the committee thought wise, but with an eye on what they thought the Rules Committee would accept. Many a bill has been reconsidered by the parent committee to satisfy the prejudices of the Rules Committee. It may be truly said that the Rules Committee is the graveyard of much legislation.

More than that, by controlling the terms of debate—the number of amendments, for example—the Rules Committee can continue to exert control even after the bill has gone to the Floor of the House. The Landrum-Griffin was such a bill, moulded substantially by control over the amendment process. Civil Rights was another, where an even tighter rein was put on the amendment process, affecting the final outcome very decidedly.

Our bill from Interior receives its Rule, and the resolution proposing it is cleared through the Majority Leader for action on the Floor. The Majority Leader, working with his opposite member on the Republican side, programs the bill for Floor action. At the designated time on the calendar, a Democratic member of the Rules

Committee rises, and receives a prearranged recognition from the Speaker. While it is technically possible to secure recognition without prearrangement, the clutter of business and the large size of the House make the orderly transaction of business almost impossible without it. Again, it may be noted, this power of recognition is another vital element of the authority of the Speaker.

The Rules Committee member says, "Mr. Speaker, I call up H. R. —— and ask for its immediate consideration." The Speaker responds, "The gentleman is recognized for one hour." (Half of this time is then allotted to a Republican member of the Rules Committee.)

The House, sitting as the House, then debates the resolution providing for the Rule on our Interior Committee bill. The congressman who controls the time for his side (Republican or Democrat) is called the "floor leader." He may parcel out his time any way he wishes to do so. The debate on the Rule is generally a summary of the issues involved and actually constitutes a prelude to the further debate which will follow.

It is a foregone conclusion that the resolution will pass. Only once in a while will it be voted down, and if it is voted down, the bill is disposed of. It is finished. This happened recently when an important member of the Appropriations Committee took the Floor to oppose the Rule on the Chesapeake Canal Park. With prestige at his back, the Rule was voted down. This is most unusual. In most instances, even if a Member is opposed to the bill, he will vote for the Rule in order to give the matter an opportunity to be debated on the Floor.

The description of the procedures in the House will be concluded with the next newsletter.

Very sincerely,

Clem Miller

Dear Friend:

This will continue our account of the progress of a bill through the House.

The stage is set for debate on the bill. This is done by the parliamentary device known as the Committee of the Whole House on the State of the Union, herein called CWH. The device arose in Stuart England in order to protect the secrecy of parliamentary debate from the king. Since that time it has become a means of providing informality and expedition to the rules and procedures of the House. Debate is freer and recognition of Members more ready. However, while the *rules* are relaxed, control is retained, perhaps augmented, by the Rules Committee's guardianship of the terms of debate—the control it exerts over ingress to CWH and egress from it.

Now that debate on the Rule has been completed on our bill, and the resolution voted favorably, the Chairman of the Interior Committee says, "Mr. Speaker, I move that the House resolve itself into the Committee of the Whole House for the State of the Union to consider H. R. ———." The Speaker then designates a congressman to act as Chairman of CWH who will preside during the debate on the bill. The chairman so designated assumes the Speaker's dais and the Speaker steps down. This too is a heritage of Stuart England when the Speaker, as the king's representative, was not welcome at the deliberations of the committee. None of the other Members of the House move at all. The change has been solely a parliamentary one.

The Democratic floor manager, usually the parent committee chairman, begins debate by setting forth the basic facts on the bill. The Republican floor manager then responds with the minority opinion. These presentations may take ten to fifteen minutes. (Since time is so limited, floor managers rarely consume more time.) Then, other Members of Congress are heard. The floor manager apportions this time very carefully, usually in five-minute blocks. Members of the parent committee are given priority, and during debate on important bills they will consume the entire allotted time. Thus, the general debate runs its course, with the timekeeper at the elbow of the Chairman of the CWH, evening up the Democratic and Republican apportionments as best he can. General debate is just that. It is the effort to persuade Members by the logic of your argument. Some speakers are good. Their arguments are direct and telling. Others seem totally ineffective, and many will produce arguments that are quite irrelevant.

The effectiveness of general debate, as persuasion, is often disputed. Good debate seems to have the effect of reinforcing your basic sympathies. It does not appear that many individual votes are changed; and even rarer is there any alteration of final results.

After general debate, the bill is then read by the Clerk, line by line. At any place a Member may propose an amendment. When the amendment has been read, the initiator has five minutes to speak on it. Any other Member may also speak on the amendment for five minutes. Note that recognition is automatic instead of at the pleasure of the Speaker.

As each amendment is proposed and debated, it is voted upon. The first vote taken is a voice vote. Any Member, but usually the originator of the amendment or its principal opponent, may ask for a "division" vote. A division vote is a standing vote, first those for the amendment, then those opposed. Alternatively, a "teller" vote may be requested. For this vote, those favoring pass through the center aisle of the Chamber between tellers, then those opposed. Neither of these voting methods records the vote by name. No roll call votes whereby the Members may be identified are taken in the CWH. This again harks back to the secret character of this historical institution.

This is most significant. Members who vote to cut the heart out of a bill with their unrecorded votes will favor the bill on final passage and publicly proclaim their affection for the terms of the bill. Members listed as economizers will vote for amendments that frequently mean billions, but then vote against final passage, knowing that others will pick up the tab to pass the bill in order that the business of government may proceed. Conversely, "spenders" will vote for amendments to save money, but get no credit for it because their only recorded vote is in favor of the over-all bill on final passage.

Theoretically, debate in CWH could be very time consuming with each Member accorded five minutes per amendment under the Rule. It rarely works out this way in practice. For a while, in any debate, the Members will put up with a long string of speakers. As time goes on, however, this willingness tends to evaporate. Low calls of "Vote, vote!" begin to come from the back of the Chamber. If debate under this five-minute rule begins to stretch on and on, the Speaker appears from nowhere at the Democratic floor manager's elbow with an angry frown on his face.

The floor manager says, "I ask unanimous consent that all debate on this amendment end in fifteen minutes." If unanimous consent is not forthcoming, he *moves* that all debate end in fifteen minutes. The temper of the House generally is such that the motion carries by voice vote with only a scattering of "nays."

At this point the fifteen minutes is then divided equally among all Members on their feet at the time. If seven are standing, each gets about two minutes.

There is a more wholesale way of cutting down on debate. The floor manager, after observing the restiveness of the Members and the lateness of the hour, may say, "I move that debate on this amendment and *all other amendments,* and all debate on this bill be ended at seven o'clock." If this motion carries, it has the effect of telescoping debate in a hurry.

Recently, at five o'clock we were on page three of a twenty-page bill. Amendments by the score were in the offing. Each amendment was getting a thorough working over under the five-minute rule. But the Members were quite impatient. A motion to end debate at six o'clock passed easily. The Members on their feet seeking recognition at the time were so numerous, they only had a minute and a half to speak on any or all amendments to be offered. At six o'clock there were still a string of amendments remaining for consideration. Under the motion all that could then be done was to read the amendments in order. Then, without debate, they were voted up or down.

After the bill has been read, the amendments voted upon, the CWH rises. No one moves from his place except the Chairman of the CWH. He steps down and his place is taken by the Speaker who calls first for separate votes on any amendment which may be desired (if the Rule permits it). If amendments which the floor managers feel are undesirable have prevailed in the CWH, a separate vote may be requested to try to knock them out. There also may be an effort to recommit the bill to its parent committee. If this fails, as it generally does, there is then a vote on final passage. This may be by voice vote or by roll call. If a roll call is desired, a fifth of the Members present (usually about fifty) must stand to support the demand. This means that much important legislation goes through without a recorded vote, and in many instances insignificant bills may be the subject of a roll-call vote. A great deal of the strategy behind the consideration of legislation is wrapped up in decisions on how and under what circumstances voting shall proceed.

In asking for a teller or roll-call vote a Member must weigh the psychological effects of putting his fellows on the spot. He must weigh the parliamentary effect if he should win (or lose) by a narrow margin (or a large margin). Subsequent events can be altered by misjudging these factors. One has only a few seconds to make up his mind to ask for a vote. It is always an electric moment when the Speaker cocks his ear on the voice vote. "In the opinion of the Chair, the ayes have it . . . the ayes have it. So ordered. A motion to reconsider is laid on the table. . . ." As the Speaker pauses, one can weigh his chances, then decide.

The purpose of this strategy may be to conceal your true strength, or it may be to make a show of force that will intimidate the opposition. Losing a teller vote may put one in a bad position to call for a roll call later. Calling for a vote at a certain point may exasperate Members to repudiate your position. As we have had occasion to remark previously, power unexpended may be more influential than power expressed.

Very sincerely,

Clem Miller

Dear Friend:

Recently we considered how legislation is pounded in or out of shape through committee action. Now, let us turn to a consideration of action on the Chamber Floor. Ordinarily, amending the committee bill on the Floor is a difficult job. Unless the stakes are high and there is a good base of political support, it is not attempted. It is too vast a place for localized action; there are too many watchdogs. The traditional deference to the authority of one of its committees overwhelms the main body. The whole fabric of Congress is based on committee expertness, and the practice of "rewriting a bill on the Floor" is thought of as a bad business. Even so, on occasion, minor amendments will slip through. More rarely, entire bills are substituted. Generally this occurs through the intensity of opposition on a major bill, but it also comes about through inattention.

"On this vote the ayes are 185, the nays are 186. The amendment is not agreed to, and the clerk will read." With these words the Administration's compromise upon a compromise of the original compromise on the Minimum Wage Bill for 1961 went down to defeat during this session. Its name: the Albert Amendment to the Kitchin-Ayres Substitute for the Roosevelt Bill. The work of months, the product of a thousand meetings, the final result of fat volumes of hearings, of yards of statistics—all left in ruins.

At this precise point in the legislative process on which we are focusing, general debate has been concluded. Now we have what is called debate under the "Five Minute Rule." The bill is read, line by line. At any point it is open to amendment. Anyone can speak for five minutes. Then, the amendment is voted up or down by voice vote, division or teller. A teller vote takes about ten minutes. This time element is crucial, because if you wish to vote you must be in attendance or very close by. There is no long roll call to give you time to hurry from your office to the Floor. Roll calls are not in order at this stage of parliamentary procedure.

To be there. That is the trick. Or, for the Leadership to get you there and keep you there. It is more difficult than it sounds!

There are over 265 Democrats in the House. A total teller vote of 300 from a House membership of 437 is a substantial vote. A vote of 185 to a side is an excellent turnout. At least 150 Members can be counted on to be absent from any teller vote.

What is it that happens to these Members of Congress? Presumably, they were elected for this very task above all others: to be in the Chamber, to vote.

The fact is that this objective is blurred with time and circumstance. So much of what occurs on the Floor is routine. There are only rare occasions when circumstances *demand* one's presence. Thus, what is of overriding significance gives way to what is immediate. The competing interests, the endless details of congressional routine, take hold. Members are called to the Floor for a quorum call as the afternoon's debate begins. Soon, nearly everyone arrives to answer his name. Most stay for a while, listening and chatting. Then, inevitably, the drift begins. Pages hurry up and down the aisles with sheaves of messages, calling a congressman to argue with an executive department on behalf of a constituent, or to tell a garden club delegation why he favors the Shasta daisy for the national flower.

Or the Member goes downstairs for lunch, or over to the Senate, or downtown to a conference. Gradually he is caught up in the inescapable workaday world of Congress. Almost without volition, he finds himself back in his office trying to keep up with the mail, interviewing and being interviewed by a stream of callers. Now, he is too far away to get back to the Floor for a teller vote.

Once away from the Chamber, he is far away. The urgency, the insistence, is gone. A million words of testimony, the results of a thousand patient meetings may be going down the drain. But it is another world from the congressional office.

To get Members to the Floor and keep them there for the right moment is the job of the whip organization. The Democratic Whip calls the zone whips representing regions throughout the country. His secretary speaks to other secretaries. Perhaps they can reach their Members; perhaps they cannot. Perhaps they care; perhaps they do not. If he is reached, the Member is told to come to the Floor for an important vote. Irritably, he shuffles the work on his desk. The call may be followed by another of even greater urgency, till he is told, "The Speaker wants to see you on the Floor *at once!*"

The key to effective whip action is timing. The Whip is on the Floor surveying the scene and weighing alternatives. He watches the Republicans to observe whether they are present in force or are hiding in the cloakroom awaiting a prearranged signal to descend on the Floor. He gauges the end of general debate and estimates the time when a vote is likely. If he puts out a call too soon, too urgently, many Members will assemble, take a quick look, and then begin to fade until there is a critical deficiency when the vote is taken. Yet, he can not defer too long, because a vote might come unexpectedly. When ten speakers might be scheduled under the Five Minute Rule, the Republicans could yank six all of a sudden and the vote would be upon us twenty minutes before it was expected and at a time when our Members are dispersed.

This means that there is no substitute for being in the Chamber all through debate under the Five Minute Rule, but it seems impossible to convince Democrats that this is so.

It takes organization. It takes discipline. And these, Democrats do not have in large measure. Discipline works in a democracy if it is understood. Indoctrination and organization are weak on the Democratic side. The Democrats don't meet to talk things over, to be persuaded, to be sold. We don't meet in caucus because Leadership fears that it would irreparably breach the tenuous links with the South.

So, we go our own way, heeding the calls or not. The Republicans caucus, lock horns, knock heads, and show up to vote in fairly disciplined order. The southerners, with their own whip system, festoon the Floor in season and out.

The results are at hand. Through inattention and lack of discipline a bill is lost. Perhaps it could not have been won in any case, but the failure is there for all to see. "Yes" became "no" and "no" became "yes." Legislation has been written on the Floor rather than in committee.

Very sincerely,

Clem Miller

CHAPTER II

DAY BY DAY WITH THE CONGRESSMAN

THE LIFE of a congressman may well be a rewarding one. It is also one that is extremely busy and trying. The hours are long and there is much time which must be spent on purely political or district matters. The high school senior class trip must be given almost undivided attention; the students must be personally conducted on a tour of the Capitol—always with the picture made on the steps for publication back in the district. Go into your congressman's office and tell his secretary that you are visiting "from the district"—you will see him almost immediately, regardless of what he is working on at the time.

A congressman must spend time with the representatives of those interest groups which make up a part of his constituency. This is true even if he does not agree with their position and probably will not vote as they desire.

He has relations of one form or the other with the press as well. The wire services and correspondents must be met and, if possible, given a favorable impression and story. To do so is not always easy, with newspaper, radio, and television deadlines demanding that interesting news be found—or, if not found, made.

A congressman's family, his home, his past and present, his utterances, and his silences are a part of the public domain and will be examined and written about. Being a congressman, in this sense, is probably more trying than being a minister's child in a small town.

But the massive problems of a busy life and a goldfish-bowl existence seem almost easy compared to the complexity of life when the congressman, and particularly the newcomer to Congress, comes into contact with the rules and precedents of Congress, the procedures which determine the kind of body it is. Woodrow Wilson, in referring to these rules, explained their nature and particularly the problems of the freshman.

. . . No man, when chosen to the membership of a body possessing great powers and exalted prerogatives, likes to have his activity repressed, and himself suppressed, by imperative rules and precedents which seem to have been framed for the deliberate purpose of making usefulness unattainable by individual members. Yet such the new member finds the rules and precedents of the House to be. It matters not to him, because it is not apparent on the face of things, that those rules and precedents have grown, not out of set purpose to curtail the privileges of new members as such, but out of the plain necessities of business; it remains the fact that he suffers under their curb, and it is not until "custom hath made it in him a property of easiness" that he submits to them with anything like good grace.[1]

This group of letters shows almost in a candid camera way various facets of the public life of a congressman and the private problems he faces in legislative activity.

[1] Woodrow Wilson, *Congressional Government*, (New York, 1885), pp. 62-63. This truly remarkable study of Congress is as up-to-date as if it had been written this year. Congress has changed little. The rules and precedents have become only more deeply rooted.

Dear Friend:

It might be profitable to venture some observations on the relationship between this newcomer to Congress and the press.

First, there is the relationship with the home district newspapers. It is distinct and different from the Washington press. By and large, it is locally oriented, and properly so.

The key to this relationship is that it is a one-way street. The exchange almost always starts at this end, the Washington end, and flows out *to* the local newspaper. It is an arms-length affair. It is dominated by the mimeographed press release, which, in my case, has to be mailed to every newspaper in the First District. Occasionally we will wire the germ of a news item to a specific newspaper; even more rarely, we will telephone the item. We face a constant problem of the dailies and the weeklies. The timing of a release is vital to the newspaper. It does not get run in the weekly if it does not arrive on the spot at the right time. With different press days, with the unpredictable timing of developments in Washington, and with our limited resources, this process of communication is difficult and often frustrating for all concerned.

The role of the newspaper is usually passive, and occasionally hostile. Their news staffs are overworked and understaffed, have very limited budgets, and receive a never-ending flood of materials from all sides. The congressman gets his due along with a thousand other competing interests. Anyway, why should the editor worry when he has a senator and a congressman competing to deliver the news to him on a silver platter. That's the fact. The senator wants his name in the paper, so he is in there with a wire early. The congressman wants his name in there, so he is on the phone. This is the system. Newspapers like it. They call it "competition," and in America we always like to see the other fellow engaged in competition. Whether this is good for the newspapers or their readers is another matter.

Newspapers at home usually see no need to check with their congressman on facts or on his position. The number of times that I have been contacted by *any* newspaper in my district in two years can be counted on the fingers of one hand.

Second, there is the relationship with the wire services, UPI and AP. At the opening of Congress in 1959 there was a brief flurry of contact from the wire service "regional men" handling California. Since then, there has been less contact. The reasons are the same. Overwork, understaffing, and the flood of news. The UPI regional man for California, for example, is expected to cover all of the representatives and senators from ten or so western states. He is also responsible for reporting developments of possible interest to his service's clients—newspapers, and radio and TV stations—from several hundred committees and subcommittees on Capitol Hill as well as Floor activity in both houses. Harry Humphries of AP has always been most agreeable to talk to me if I call him. He will come around to the office and talk about it. But newsworthy occasions never seem to arise. The twist or angle which would make it news does not seem to be present. The effect of this is that constituents do not generally know what their congressman is doing, nor do they have a chance to find out. What is "news"? What is newsworthy in America today? Are the views of a congressman on current legislation, his voting record, etc., "news" to his constituency? Apparently not. I feel frustrated to the extent that I make little effort to promote this sort of thing, and conversely, little effort is made to elicit it from me by newsmen.

A third category is one which might be described as the national press corps, the newsmen responsible for telling America what goes on in Washington and Congress. There is a large gallery immediately over the Speaker's chair reserved for the press. It is generally devoid of occupants. Except for crowded state occasions, there may be only one, two, or three newsmen bird-dogging the proceedings below. By and large, the reporting is quite perfunctory with little of the shading which gives political life its validity. While I believe this is unfortunate, it is understandable. The press has no time for shading today. This is the "age of the headline" and the "news capsule." Headlines come from the White House or from Senator Johnson's office, rarely from congressional debate. Congressman Chester Bowles made a foreign policy address last year. Not a line of the speech was reported by the press. Ditto for a speech by Senator Engle on our China policy. Another important speech on domestic economy was buried at the bottom of some other pronouncement. I suppose lapses like this can be defended because the timing was wrong or the speaker didn't get enough copies of the speech to the galleries, or because the general level of debate in the House is so low that the gold nugget was overlooked, etc., etc.

Sometimes, however, even by its own standard of judgment about news, the press fails. Such a major failure, to my way of thinking, was exemplified by the lack of coverage of the attempt by the Chairman of the Rules Committee to chastise a congressman for a critical radio broadcast. For the first time in a decade the subsurface feud between northern Democrats and the Rules Committee majority broke out into the open. It may well prove to herald an historic turning point in the development of the House of Representatives. Yet, there was not a line, *not a line,* of this "effort to censure" in the newspapers the following day. A complete blackout. Was this due to inattentiveness on the part of the press? I do not know. What I do know is that it was a deplorable failure to report what I consider significant news—news that would inform and would promote understanding. So concerned is the press with the surface events of the day that the meaning of life in Washington is many times all but obscured or actually distorted beyond resemblance. The best case in point is the novel *Advise and Consent* which is full of surface but tells little about congressional politics.

It also means that some news gets lost. An interesting example comes to mind. Everyone was interested in what the congressional Democratic landslide of 1958 would produce. No radical changes materialized and the press lost interest. When the Democratic Study Group was formed in the House in September, 1959, the event went unreported. Prominent members of the press told me all through 1960 that the DSG was a flash in the pan. It would not survive, so it was not worth attention. However, lately a series of visitors not connected with newspapers have been coming to my office to talk about the DSG. The talk is discursive, ruminative, and stimulating. In various smaller periodicals, articles are now appearing about it. As yet, not one of the major news media or their interpretative writers has had a line published about this development. This is some indication of the news gap.

How the press gallery functions, I do not have the faintest idea. This is perhaps an admission of deficiency on my part. It is worth reporting only as illustrative of the chasm which exists between one junior congressman and the press.

If the press did not report Congress, Congress could hardly function. If the sound of congressional voices carried no farther than the bare walls of the Chambers, Congress could disband. We know this; it is brought home to us every day. Reporters appear very aware of their powers. From where I sit, it is a power they are not backward about using.

This suggests a basic rivalry between the press corps and congressmen. I must confess that I feel it. To the wise old birds in the Press Gallery, we politicians are trying to put something over on somebody. Exposure of this public show by politicians is a major portion of the routine of the newspaperman's job, and I agree it must be an important part. There is a tendency to fatuousness and fat-headedness which must be restrained. To the congressman, however, publicity is his lifeblood. It is his career, his fate, and it brings an emotion to his relationship with the press which the newsman does not comprehend, but which he can manipulate—very frequently with too much enjoyment to be bearable.

A good case in point was a recent newspaper series on nepotism which won its author a Pulitzer Prize. To my knowledge there was no news sleuthing carried on with more vigor than this investigation into the family members on congressional pay rolls. It was carried on in the finest traditions of the journalistic profession. It was a joyous rousting-about of the rascally politician. Actually, it shed little light, it contributed little. It was harmful, I believe, to the public's understanding of Congress. This should not be construed as the favoring of nepotism, but there was no effort to tell the other side—the great financial difficulties which many congressmen operate under in doing their jobs. It killed for this session the addition of a staff man to each office, badly needed indeed under congressional loads presently carried by most of us.

Then, there was the famous *Life* exposé of expense accounts. What enthusiasm this engendered! There was another side to this story also that was never told. The main point I am seeking to make is that much of the press seems to regard its Washington role as it does police reporting. The broader sweep of the meaningful "why" and the "wherefore" of government is lost in the welter of what is on the police captain's blotter.

At a newspapermen's dinner one night I was the only politician present. The talk was all about the trade—and to this outsider it was fascinating indeed. After dinner the talk got on to campaigns, and I made a few tentative assertions with suitable disclaimers of infallibility. Immediately I became the subject of a biting cross-examination by one of those present. There was no intention to be rude or discourteous, but I became uncomfortable and distracted. There was some unwitting contempt—this gentleman from the press was on the highest level and knew all. There was some real enjoyment on his part about what a monkey I was. He leaned back, arms akimbo, gallus-snapping. He was supremely happy, putting a congressman in his place. It was all quite unconscious and unintentional, and he would have been mortified if I had told him of the impression he made. I was quite angry, even so. This was a social event, not an inquisition.

Finally, there is the relationship with a host of national correspondents who are busy explaining in their signed columns and interpretative articles what the newspapers seem unable to do in the news columns. I see these men closeted with the committee chairmen in the Speaker's Lobby. I am introduced to them occasionally. I have had dinner with them and found them delightful.

I have talked to them in the Speaker's Lobby, but it is difficult for me to talk to newspapermen. I don't seem to have the hang of it. I don't like to talk in clichés and the headline phrase does not come easily. Since the press operates under terrifying time pressures, many newsmen think in clichés. They want congressmen to talk in clichés. They become uneasy if you tend toward too much "background" talk, or if your thoughts are tentative. This, of course, is due to the modern demand for slogans. Everything is compressed. People have no time to attend, to listen. We have become a nation of headline readers. It is not at all surprising that the working press has come to require the same of politicians in its day-to-day reporting. The result is distortion, the inevitable distortion that comes from oversimplification and compression.

This is not to absolve myself. The job of a congressman, in major degree, is communicating—making our political world understandable. By dealing too much in the "grey" area of political life, and not presenting sharp, didactic alternatives, I do not make the job easier. I am constantly striving to do this, but my concept of the real political world does not make for an easy fit.

There are reporters who seek background. It is hard to get the knack of talking "background," "off-the-record," "on-the-record," unless you have a firm idea of the ground rules. Reporters become frustrated by the congressman who does not know the ground rules, who switches back and forth from "off-the-record" to "on-the-record," who interlards his talk with trivia or philosophy. The reporter's standard reaction to this sort of thing is to turn off his traveling pencil.

What all this means in terms of Congress is that the congressman who tailors his speech and remarks to the strictures of modern reporting is going to get in the news; and he who doesn't is going to have difficult sledding. It means that many capable legislators operate fairly silently, while others who might be of inferior competence are heard from quite frequently.

Very sincerely,

Clem Miller

Dear Friend:

In the spirit of "equal time" I have asked William Broom of Ridder Publications, a good friend and highly able Washington correspondent, to respond to my last newsletter which, you will remember, discussed the relationship between the Washington press corps and freshmen congressmen. His response is as follows:

A NEWSPAPERMAN LOOKS AT A FRESHMAN CONGRESSMAN

"Newspapermen and politicians are natural enemies—mostly because they need each other.

"The enmity is strictly impersonal. It comes about because a politician prefers to say what he wishes the public and his constituents to hear. Of necessity, a newspaperman must ask questions that require him to say more than that.

"More often than not, newsmen and politicians become personal friends. This usually happens when the politician understands that the newsman is interested not in what he says or stands for, but in what he does and whether it serves the interest of most of the people who elected him.

"In short, excluding demagogues no matter how skillful they may be, we care less what the man advocates than we do how well he advocates. This explains why a newsman can be equally fond of a Hubert Humphrey and a Robert Taft.

"This is the lesson every newspaperman tries gently to teach the freshman congressman when he first arrives in Washington. Some congressmen never learn it. They're the ones who don't last long. Frequently, they are also the ones who complain of unfair treatment by the press.

"It is no accident that the Washington press corps labels first-term congressmen "freshmen" instead of "first-termers" or some other equally descriptive title. They're freshmen because they have so much to learn.

"The first thing a freshman congressman must learn is that he's pretty small potatoes in Washington. This is a painful lesson for the man who has just been given "a mandate from the people" in a district of several hundred thousand citizens.

"The freshman arrives, starry-eyed and out to save the nation from disaster, and where does he find himself? He finds himself in twenty-first place on the official protocol list, right behind former Vice-Presidents and just ahead of the Undersecretary of State. (Also outranking him: the Director of the Budget and the Assistant to the President.)

"Unless some unusual political circumstance or personal qualification exists, he also finds himself assigned to a committee that hasn't the remotest connection with the major interest of his district.

"The freshman is quickly disabused of the notion that he can arise in the House of Representatives during a debate and deliver himself of a thought so impelling that it will be reported on every front page in the nation, igniting a conflagration in the minds of men everywhere. He finds that most speeches are limited to five minutes, three minutes, or even one minute.

"Can he sit back and listen to the debate, and then, after intensive research and inner struggle, judiciously cast his vote? He can, but it may cost him a seat on a better committee or the appropriation for that flood control project back in his district if his vote doesn't follow the party leadership.

"Still reeling from these discoveries, the freshman to his dismay finds that his fate often rests in the hands of strangers—the staff members he employs, an assistant secretary in one of the executive departments, a committee chairman or senior congressman whose advice he seeks. If he's a good judge of people, and if he understands himself and what he believes in, he may end up getting more from these strangers than they do from him.

"The freshman may arrive consumed with interest in the great national and international issues. After he's answered the pile of mail from his constituents, he may have an hour left to consider them or inform himself about the big issues. For it is an unfortunate fact that as the federal government continues to expand its functions, the congressman finds himself more and more a pleader of special problems and a prisoner of the mailbox.

"Confronted by those dismal circumstances, the freshman arouses mixed emotions in the newsman. His predicament deserves and gets sympathy. A minority deserve admiration. They get it when they work their way into re-election, to a better committee job, or to a position of stature and respect among other congressmen.

"Seldom does the newsman pity the first-termer because, as sure as the night follows the day, every freshman wants to become a sophomore."

Very sincerely,

Clem Miller

Dear Friend:

Here follows, in answer to numerous (at least three) requests, an account of the way I spend a typical day. I arise at 6:45, eat breakfast, and spend ten minutes with the *Washington Post*, skimming the news and reading the editorials and columns. Leave for the office at 7:55 A.M., arriving at congressional parking lot at 8:20 A.M. (Alternatively, I may breakfast at 8:00 A.M. with a veterans group, Boy Scouts or some other group—Thursday last, with the British Ambassador. I enjoyed good conversation with a British Member of Parliament and three other congressmen, and had a chance to do a little indirect complaining about the legislative program, under the guise of social discussion. Breakfast seems to be the best time of day to talk to someone seriously.)

Back at the office, your congressman is at the desk from 8:30 to 10:00 A.M. at least, or possibly till 12:30 P.M. First off, I look at the mail, perhaps a carry-over from the preceding day, dictating replies, and stashing aside the reports, memos, mimeographs, speeches, publicity blurbs, brochures, for later study. The average daily onslaught of mail, excluding newspapers, makes a stack about fourteen inches high.

Generally, at 9:00 comes the first office appointment: A trade association to discuss an industrial problem, or a lobbyist to explain his position on a bill. I invite them to come in. Right now, I am wrestling mightily with the problem of what to do about fair trade laws. I invite interested parties to meet with me and discuss their point of view. I have just recently concluded a similar study on the Administration's proposals for taxing cooperatives.

At 10:00, there may well be a hearing of the committee to which I am assigned, or of the subcommittee currently holding extensive hearings on the depressed areas bill. One of our major problems consists of getting to our committee hearings on time. Frequently it seems almost impossible to arrive on time for these hearings, what with the press of office work. However, the committee work is vital to the work of Congress, and I think it well-nigh a national disgrace to observe witnesses who have traveled many miles speaking to a committee of one member. So, I make it a point to be there on time.

The House meets at 12:00 noon. Usually, it is in session four or five days a week. Members are rather erratic in their attendance. If there is a debate on a bill, I will generally be there.

Fitting lunch into this schedule often becomes difficult. Frequently I have luncheon engagements. Frankly, I do not have time for them. I usually eat at my office, and relax with a newspaper from the state capital or my district.

Then, during afternoon hours, I am busy cramming committee meetings between duties on the Floor or in the office. Yesterday, for instance, several of us had a 2:00 P.M. meeting with John K. Galbraith on tight money and economic policy. The debate over Hawaiian statehood was also on and I listened to that for a while. Then, a meeting with a member of the Appropriations Committee on our district public works.

About 5:00 P.M. I return to the office to work over the mail, sign letters, and see people. Getting away from the office is more and more difficult. In the beginning, I left at 5:45 P.M. Now I am leaving at 6:15 or 6:30 P.M.

Evenings I spend at home as much as possible. A congressman can eat out five and six nights a week if he wishes to. After having attended several functions, I have now cut them down to a minimum. I have been invited to dinner with the assurance that it is "strictly social." However, the socializing is somewhat difficult and quite flat. The feeling will not down that behind the tenderloin steak is the cold and indifferent practicality of the Washington lobby. So, I tell the inviters "no." Instead, I invite them to my office to speak frankly about their problems. I learn more faster, and feel better.

At night, after supper, I read another district paper as well as the reports, speeches, and magazines that have accumulated during the day. I throw some out, keep others for filing, and separate others for condensing on five-by-eight cards.

About 11:00 or 12:00 P.M. the day is at an end. I like to top it off with a chapter from a book. This is a busy day, six days a week. I present it to you neither for commiseration nor vainglory. I like it. It is very lively, and may some day be rewarding. (I hope the account may prove instructive, and helpful without being sickly. Each of us has his own tolerance in this department.)

Very sincerely,

Clem Miller

Dear Friend:

I have been asked "How do congressmen get along? How do the parties get along?" It is difficult to generalize, but there is clearly a restraint. A fellow congressman from my state who is of the opposite party rides down in the elevator. As we get off at the same floor, he scoots away; no chance for joining him in the walk back to the office.

Another time, I walked back through the subway with two fellows from my state, one who had just concluded a strong speech for the Un-American Activities Committee, the other an old foe of the committee. Where was the common ground? They agreed on changing the name of the committee, the liberal suggesting that with this change it might also alter its objective. They agreed also that the Supreme Court's Watkins decision made change necessary. What else? The liberal indicated that techniques have changed since Martin Dies. An agreement by the committee defender that there was indeed room for improvement. And, as we walked along, a tentative, wary search for some agreement. As the liberal turned off, I continued on with the defender. He stared at me quite candidly. Not unfriendly. So I had taken Hubert's place? I would like it in Congress. I longed to ask him whether he really thought those disagreeing with him were fools or knaves—but instead I asked if he preferred his fifth-floor office. Yes, he said smiling, throwing out his hand expressively.

Next time we met, a curt, hard nod, as we stood silently together in an elevator.

Very sincerely,

Clem Miller

Dear Friend:

During my recent trip through the district, I talked about many things. In line with my policy that the first duty of a congressman is to the area he represents, I attempted to make meaningful reports relating to the everyday concerns of the group I was addressing. I spoke of conservation, recreation, and lumber, and of the overriding necessity for these seeming disparate interests to join toward solving their common problem: the best and highest use of our public lands. I talked of harbor development. I usually referred to atomic energy, and to my feeling that we are bungling this tremendous force for peace or war. I spoke of our defense establishment and of the possibilities for tremendous savings, particularly through unification of many tasks.

I talked of the proliferation of government—at all levels—because of these twin circumstances: our exploding population and rapidly advancing technology. I tried to relate to specific problems: pollution control, traffic signals for land and sky, man-made lakes, chemical warfare against weeds and bugs, the urbanization of this country. And always we discussed "tight money" and its relation to inflation, to monetary and fiscal policy.

Then, I generally spoke of the coming session of Congress. I said I saw aid to education as our top priority legislative need. Next, an increase in the minimum wage to $1.25 an hour, and revision of the 1958 Atomic Energy Act. Then there is the need for loophole-closing tax reform, and the current monumental investigation of our entire tax system by the House Ways and Means Committee. I usually referred to the coming breakthrough in a nation-wide natural resource conservation policy (perhaps not this year, but imperative for the near future).

I tried to report congressional realities as seen by a new Member. Several times, before sympathetic audiences, I tried to define the limits of congressional abilities, and never with particular success. People simply did not want to hear, for example, that the role of Congress in foreign policy is largely passive, one of reaction to Executive action. It is not that I have no ideas on foreign policy. (I have gone so far as to set down a ten-point program.) But foreign policy is largely outside the constitutional scope of Congress, especially of the House. As I say, people did not want to hear this. They actively rejected it. It is as though they were saying, "You are our representative in Congress. We expect you to assert your views. We expect action. We expect Congress to lead and mold opinion."

This dilemma was thrown into sharp relief by a TV newscaster (a neighbor) who was helping me to develop "presence" before the TV camera. He asked, "What kind of an image do you want to project? Do you just want to be a *good* congressman? Or do you want to be a national oracle, speaking as the great voice of experience from Washington? They are different you know." Then he mentioned Congressman X. "He's going to be the next senator from ——." I sat back in stunned silence. Congressman X a senator? But the more I thought about it, the more likely it seemed. X appears indifferent to his low congressional standing as he reaches for a national audience. People need symbols to reflect their aims.

It cannot be said, of course, that Congress cannot and should not exercise some restraining or encouraging hand on the Executive. There is a degree of influence. Witness recent hearings of the foreign relations committees of House and Senate. In this, we stand in much the same relationship to the Executive as a citizen does to his representatives—to restrain or exhort.

During and after meetings in the district, I was asked, "What influence do I have?" "What can I do to help?" "Do you read your correspondence?" Certainly, in the round, public opinion is decisive. How decisive varies with the congressman and the legislation, and the nature of the appeal. My counsel to everyone who asked was to write. One letter might spark an entirely new line of thought or endeavor. I can think of several issues last session upon which particular letters gave me a fresh or definitive focus.

Letters in aggregate may help to resolve congressional thinking. Every vote must be a consensus. Therefore, it must be a resolution of many stimuli. Sometimes a volume of mail seems to force an issue to a conclusion without seeming to have any particular effect on the actual result. The Labor Bill is a good case in point. The agitation for *a* labor bill pushed the House Committee on Education and Labor to take *some* sort of action. Our mail was not much help in deciding exactly *what* should be done. The congressional mail bore a doubtful relationship to the bill which actually resulted. Because of the parliamentary ins and outs, the complexities of the field, and the emotional involvement of the "experts" on both sides, most of the mail gave us little help. Most useful at such times are direct, first-person factual accounts of constituents' own personal experiences. This is the most difficult letter to write, because the humdrum of our lives cannot be seen as pulse and excitement for the nonparticipant.

On other types of legislation, heavy mail in aggregate seems to exert some influence. On the bill to permit self-employed persons to defer taxes on certain retirement funds, the sudden volume of mail, descending all at once, with no adverse mail, seemed to make passage a certainty. It tended to resolve any doubts one might have. And, indeed, the bill did pass with a thumping majority.

In my mind, the lobby is one of the best ways an individual citizen may participate in his government. To many this seems repugnant. First, there is lobbying's reputation. Second, it is still an indirect, rather than direct, form of participation. Third, a particular lobby may be a poor instrument, may misrepresent itself, may actually subvert the wishes of many of those supporting it.

However, the lobby is still probably the best means of approaching Congress. A good lobby, with its technical resources, can speak to a congressman on his own terms. It is not diverted by irrelevancies, and if it is, then it is not a good lobby. A good lobbyist is one who knows his legislative objectives, who has the facts firmly in hand, who can separate the facts from his prejudices, and proceed to the matter at hand with directness.

Congress is very large, and this makes most lobbies skeletal affairs with a tendency to substitute public relations "hoorah" and slick paper and shadows on the wall for legwork and reasoned persuasion.

Even within the limits a lobby may set for itself, it may do a job that is more harmful to its clients than helpful.

The purposes of this letter will be served if I am understood to suggest that many citizens may best help themselves legislatively if they will select those organizations which represent their aspirations and then back them with some of their treasure to carry forward the work.

Very sincerely,

Clem Miller

Dear Friend:

The congressional recess is that period in the fall, after adjournment, which offers respite from the steady press of legislation. Congressmen, extremely weary of themselves and their fellows, are eager to be home—to see how things are.

Congress remains in session for longer and longer periods as the complexity of government mounts. In the early days of the republic, sessions lasted from one to three months. Today, a nine-or-ten-month session is routine.

Recess at home is traditionally a time for checking grass-roots reaction; it is also a time for public viewing of the congressman. Citizens have a right to see their representative, to talk to him and observe him.

In a city district, a central office with daily office hours is sufficient. In a district covering as much territory as the First California (if transplanted to the East Coast it would reach from Boston to Baltimore), this is impossible.

As soon as I know about when Congress will adjourn, my field representative and I frame in certain dates from the requests for appearances which come in to us. We spot invitations on the calendar, providing a schedule that will move us from one community to another, in a sequential manner. A great deal of time must be spent actually on the road. Our station wagon is loaded with files of research material, congressional reports to distribute to constituents, and all the personal paraphenalia we need for a two-month safari —including cookstove and stenographic recording equipment.

My home and office for two or three months is a series of motels. The pressure of the schedule and the distances involved make use of my real home in Corte Madera impossible.

We usually begin with three or four days in Marin County with headquarters in a San Rafael motel, ready for engagements in nearby towns.

From Marin, we move to my district office in Santa Rosa in reach of various Sonoma County towns. Then, a swing north along Highway 101, from Ukiah to Cresent City. Returning, we tour through

Lake County, into the Napa Valley, and back to Marin to prepare for a renewal of the cycle. Such a swing around the 300-mile-long district takes at least 10 days and preferably 15 to 18 days. Two such complete swings are made during a recess, with side forays into smaller communities. Time is set aside to talk to a dozen federal and state agencies in San Francisco and Sacramento.

We lay out the schedule with reasonable attention to population densities, and allot time for the ordinary continuing duties of a congressman. This time out for routine duties is important. The continuing duties of a Member of Congress—answering the mail from constituents, seeing individuals on special problems, and keeping up with events—do not come to a halt simply because you are on the road. The press of the routine is insistent, and must somehow be sandwiched in between service club speeches, church socials, local group barbeques, and visits to defense installations.

When we first begin a tour, the commitments are well spaced out. But as time goes on, the schedule becomes choked with a succession of extra events that make each day tighter and tighter. Telephone calls begin to follow us around from place to place. Can I spare a few minutes on this? Can I see that person for five minutes? Can I talk to the annual meeting of the Soil Conservation District directors? It may mean skimping on lunch, shaving travel time, and postponing bedtime, but we generally work them in.

A recent typical day went like this: At 7 o'clock or 8, breakfast with a small group to talk over a legislative program on dairy products for school lunches. The next engagement was set for 10 o'clock in a nearby town to talk to the high school civics class. The ample time allotted to get there was cut to ribbons by the fact that a constituent had driven up from San Rafael to see me about a harbor project. The worked-in appointment for 20 minutes took 40, so the daily rush was on—behind schedule already.

The civics class ended at 10:50; we had planned time for the drive to another town and time to collect my thoughts and make a few notes for a Rotary luncheon speech. However, the schedule did not provide for the senior problems class which blocked my exit from school with some very serious questions, demanding answers. The principal also wanted a word about science equipment available through the National Defense Education Act. According to the schedule I should have left at 11:30, but the final breakaway came 15 minutes later.

Service club luncheons you can count on. They must be over by 1:30. This gave from 1:45 to 2:45 to work on the backlog of accumulated telephone calls. (They come from everywhere. Invariably, the caller begins, "Well, you *are* a hard man to track down . . .") While I was telephoning, a delegation of Indians arrived to talk to me about their reservation hospital. At 3 o'clock I accompanied the Board of Supervisors to inspect the site of a much needed river levee to keep back floods; this took longer than anticipated. So it was a strain to arrive clean and ready for a veterans' dinner at 6:30. I had been asked to speak for 20 minutes on veterans' legislation and national defense. A part of the meal was given over to reviewing that portion of my portable file pertaining to these subjects, and to formulating notes on my remarks. This was accompanied by frequent interruptions to shake hands and to be introduced to new friends. I had to finish the dinner, the speech, and move on for an 8:30 meeting at the local farm center to discuss the farm bill. We arrived at 9 after a hectic nighttime drive over a strange road. The meeting lengthened with lively and forceful questions until 11; the room was hot and crowded. The tone of the meeting at the start had been quite hostile. At the end, as mutual understanding grew closer, the extra cake and twentieth cup of coffee (for the day) was hard to refuse. The relief of the group as tensions relaxed was obvious, and their friendly attention was hard to break away from. They followed us to the car and talked while the engine ran. Finally, we were off and down the road, with the necessity of driving to a neighboring town to position myself for the next day. Bedded down at last, the last half hour of the day was spent reading mail, a newspaper or two, and a memo from Washington in order to keep up with what was going on in my own office there and in the world, and then lights out.

This is the schedule for more than two months, seven days a week. It is a life of constant movement and relentless physical activity. It imposes a constant vigilance, unrelieved, hour upon hour. An inappropriate off-hand remark, misplaced flippancy, or a flash of irritation are not readily forgiven. People ask meaningful, serious questions on all conceivable subjects and they demand and are entitled to informed, thoughtful answers. This means an ever-active brain. Even a social evening is turned into a mental exercise. The time for solitude, for refueling of the machine, is nonexistent. As representative, I am constantly exposed to the represented—to our mutual education and benefit.

What the recess trip home also means is that my capacity, as any congressman's, is taxed to the limit. We are called on in this field of legislation one moment, in another the next moment, and a third shortly afterward.This is in the approved tradition of the United States. It is a kind of testing which Americans insist on. We use it as a yardstick for off-years as well as election years. It's an exhilarating experience but an exhausting one. The long hours of work in Washington, keeping oneself up to the mark on district and national and world affairs, pay off. When I return to Washington I know that I have been through the mill. I have sheaves of notes for action on new proposals: a mental health bill, an upgrading in priority of a proposed harbor project, a new outlook on the civil defense and shelter programs, the need for a new post office, and on and on. . . . A rest of several weeks is in order, then a new session of Congress, and I'm off again.

Very sincerely,

Clem Miller

Dear Friend:

From time immemorial, the Capitol cloakrooms have been the source of congressional policy and near-policy. At least, that is what we are told. Like the necromancer's lamp, all manner of nefarious stratagems are said to billow out of these rooms. Since rumor has it so, it is worth a look.

The first thing to know about a Capitol cloakroom is that there are no cloaks, and no place to hang one, no place for coats, umbrellas or galoshes. Congressmen are interior-oriented. They never arrive coated at the Capitol, and this is one way to detect officialdom during inclement weather. With underground passages to carry us everywhere, coats and coverings are always left at the office. So —the cloakroom contains not a peg or a stand.

The congressional cloakrooms are L-shaped appendages in each of two corners of the House Chamber, one for Republicans and one for Democrats. One arm of the cloakroom is about the size of a railroad car, with leather seats and couches arranged along an aisle, overcast with some of the least comforting ochre paint yet to grace a windowless interior. The other arm of the "L" is lined solid with a double row of telephone booths, and a snack bar where empty congressmen may stand up to eat hot dogs, ice cream bars, and soft drinks.

The cloakroom is a very private place. Pages and attendants jealously guard the entryway to the Floor of the House, and eager pages flank the openings to the cloakroom itself. Like street merchants, they vie for attention, offering service and calling to you ostentatiously by name.

Pages and attendants are there to serve, and serve they do with an eagerness that is quite overwhelming and sometimes disconcerting in its intensity. Pages are indefatigable and ingenious in finding answers large or small for congressmen. On the run, on the double, they infest the approaches to the cloakroom, imparting a bustle to one end in curious contrast to the clubby atmosphere of the other side, with its deep leather seats, and its quiet air.

As in many very private places, weighty policy seems seldom a topic. There are freighted, private discussions, *sotto voce,* that do go on, but this is not the general run. It is rather a place of escape from the ceaseless press of business; a place of refuge from the insistent and the importunate. Talk among the leather couches is general banter, idle trivia of the most ordinary sort. Everyone finds his way to the leather seats of the cloakroom at one time or another for a moment's respite, to collect and compose himself. To some it is an accustomed station, where they will repair with friends to talk endlessly of remembrances past. Interspersed among the regular is the occasional visitor who sits quietly listening, bemused by the steady flow of gossip. Periodically, one of our own showmen will put on an act, reliving a memorable hearing, or an adventure with a famous general, or a practical joke on a fellow congressman.

One absorbs the feeling that this is quite the ordinary America with its narrowness, its humanity, its immediacy.

The other face of Congress, the official face, lies around the corner of the cloakroom. There are the banks of telephones with their flashing lights, phones that are busy endlessly while Congress is in session. This is the link with the outside world. It is the ceaseless reminder that a congressman's job is communication—he is tied inextricably almost every waking moment with a message center somewhere. Pages scurry about with the messages these phones bring in. They peer here and there in every cranny of the House looking for Congressman X wanted by wheel Y in town Z. And the booths are full of serious congressmen, intent and totally involved. Faces in study and concern, gleaning, receiving, transmitting, informing—this is the congressman at his business.

There you have the congressional cloakroom, its twin halves making up the face of a congressman—coatless, hatless, and himself. On the one side, composed, relaxed and passive, on the other a relentless message center for all that is the life-stream of our country.

Very sincerely,

Clem Miller

Dear Friend:

The opening day of Congress is a time of great excitement and ferment. During the off season, Capitol Hill simmers along, hardly a ripple breaking the empty silences of the long halls and passageways. Opening day is moving day. A vast game of musical chairs takes place as some congressmen move out of their offices and newcomers move in. Restless senior congressmen with priority move from one floor to another. Furniture heaps up in the hall while squads of painters renovate whole rooms in a matter of minutes among secretaries stolidly sorting through mounds of mail.

The matter of room assignment is the jealously guarded privilege of seniority. The matter of furniture is a vital symbol of status. The exact desk. The proper chairs. The perquisites of public office are relatively few in number so that the capture of a special desk seems quite important.

When the buzzers sound for the opening call of the House the corridors begin to seethe, people emerge from everywhere—pageboys, clerks, and attendants of all sorts bustle here and there. Everyone moves a bit faster. You feel good. You feel friendly toward everyone. It's like the first day of school; it seems brand new and hopeful. When you shake hands, you mean it. You may not know the man very well. But he, too, is back from "the district."

Congressmen flood into the tunnel that connects the offices with the Capitol. The hubbub is fierce. A booming jollity. Everywhere hands are grabbed. They set off smartly in platoons of four and six, waves of men and women proceeding along the gentle incline. Deep smiles of greeting, halloos, and backslapping.

This may appear to outsiders as part of the ordinary political spectacle, the general overfriendliness of the trade; but it is much more than that. The emotions are real. The affection is a heartfelt display. It is the camaraderie of the shared experience. These people, these congressmen, have all been through the mill. They have returned from the indifferent cruelties of the political wars. They may have been saddened by the failure of friends to understand, as much as they were outraged by the indignities suffered from their opponents. Elections are unrelenting and painful. The public image of the thick-skinned politico is an inaccurate stereotype which conceals private feelings. So, the freshly-painted office, the familiar furniture, the trusted staff, their fellow ambulants, constitute a refuge, warm, friendly, understanding.

They are really glad to see one another. As the Members come piling into the Chamber through the glass door, the Reading Clerk must pause time and again for the clamor to subside. He smiles indulgently and quite happily as he nods to familiar faces. There is no great effort to keep order amid the surging throng. People squirm in their seats to greet friends. There is zip and crackle to the "hellos" ringing about the room.

The greetings on the Floor extend across the aisle to the Republican side, perhaps a trifle less effervescent, but the warmth is there. The camaraderie of the return is bipartisan. The harsh words which divide the two parties are for the moment put aside and rendered impersonal. He was not *my* opponent. He did not call *me* that. The bitterness is shelved in the joy of reunion.

The Members crowd in on the Floor, piling up along the side aisles, packing together, overflowing in front of the Speaker's dais, chattering and gesticulating, gradually finding seats. The southerners take their accustomed places in the center, the northerners along the edges. Everything is customary, familiar. The Clerk of the House calls the House to order under the rules. As the names of the Members are called by states, the cliché goes round and round—"Well, boy, it's official, you're on the payroll now!" Somberly, patiently, the teller records the vote for Speaker: each Democrat for Rayburn, every Republican for Halleck, 258-170. Mr. Speaker, Mr. Sam Rayburn, marches firmly and stolidly to the seat he has held so long, and Halleck, accompanying him to the dais, delivers the accustomed sententious amenities.

It is Speaker Rayburn's birthday. Curious how angular and grim in profile, so broad and rather complex in full face. He remains stolid and dignified throughout, stirring to smile-traces when the chairman of an important committee, his implacable legislative foe, rises to speak his words of congratulations.

You search the Speaker's face for some sign as former Speaker

Joe Martin rises. Martin leans heavily on his cane, his words are slow and full, deep affection showing through their formality. The Chamber is silent, each of us pondering what is between these two, while Martin talks throatily of long, long ago. He speaks from the center of the Chamber, next to the Democratic side, away from Minority Leader Halleck, who had succeeded to his place. Martin, the silent, is speaking to his friend, Sam Rayburn:

Mr. Speaker, and my colleagues, it is a great privilege to have the opportunity, even for a few moments, to pay my respects to a dear friend, an old friend and a Member whose friendship has lasted over 35 years without a jarring note. It has been my privilege to know Sam Rayburn all these years, and I can testify, as few men can testify, to his rugged Americanism, his loyalty to country, and his intense desire above everything else to maintain the high honor and integrity of the House of Representatives. . . .

Rayburn's face never flinches, but he shifts his weight heavily from one side to the other, cups his jaw in one and then the other hand, as he looks unblinkingly at his friend Joe Martin.

The Speaker's acceptance is restrained, stripped of all histrionics, with the simple resonance of his voice carrying his feeling. When he says "the House of Representatives has been my life, and it is today and always has been my love," it brims with emotion. One perceives from these words why he had been Speaker for twenty years. When he says

. . . I feel a deep sense of humility, because my talents are not beyond those of the average Member of the House or the average American citizen. They are all good folks; and I know that when they are geared to having faith and confidence in you, you are the only one who can destroy that faith and confidence. . .

—when he says these words you understand why he gets the allegiance of that disparate mixture called the Democratic Members of the House of Representatives. He does have faith in people. His roots are deep in the humanitarian Populist tradition of the West.

It is this faith which enables him to bridge the gap between the Texas of 1913 and the national prospect of 1961. And then he says:

I make no promise except to say that every man and woman in this House will be treated like every other Member of the House and have all the rights of every other Member of the House, because you are chosen by the people, you are a selected group. There is not a district in this country where many men and women would not like to sit where you sit today and would run against you any time they thought they could defeat you either in the primary or in the general election.

When he says this he lines up with every Member of the House personally. He is not an institution. He is not Speaker. He is one of us.

Very sincerely,

Clem Miller

Dear Friend:

The Speaker's dais stands six feet above the well of the House, and furnishes the fulcrum for life in the House. The Speaker sits a great deal at his broad desk. He may bend to some paper work, pince-nez incongruously astride his nose, scratching his signature. This is infrequent. More generally, with his great head up and thrust forward, he looks steadily around the room, resembling nothing so much as a great searchlight. Or his head may be turned aside, staring soberly down at a congressman or aide. The stance of the consultant is always the same. One foot on the level of the Speaker, one foot on the rise below, stretched forward as a supplicant—eager, attentive.

Spread out before him, the work of the House flows on in seemingly effortless streams. Things are agreed to, other things referred, others passed over. But behind the seeming effortlessness is careful planning, accommodation, compromise, checking, and clearing.

"Mr. Speaker, I ask unanimous consent for the immediate consideration of H. R. 1960 . . ." To secure that innocent sounding, "unanimous consent," a great machine has come into play. "Mr. Speaker, I offer a privileged resolution and ask for its immediate consideration." . . . "Mr. Speaker, by direction of the Committee on Rules, I call up House Resolution —— and ask for its immediate consideration . . ." The Majority Leader must know of it. Likewise, the Minority Leader. Also, the chairman of the committee involved and the ranking minority member. Then a word with the parliamentarian, always at the Speaker's right. And finally, the Speaker. He wants to know, instanter, has it been cleared all the way up the line? The Speaker hesitates for a fraction as he inwardly appraises the request. And suddenly he has assented to recognize the Member from the Floor.

Woe to the Member who has failed to clear matters properly. Both parties have an elaborate apparatus that will halt the consent action. From out of nowhere can come objections. "Mr. Speaker, I ask unanimous consent that this bill be passed over without prejudice. . . ." "Mr. Speaker, I object. . . ." The Speaker's anger flares in punctuated, sarcastic tones. "It was my understanding the gentleman had cleared this matter with other Members involved?" This is serious business in a world where so great a percentage of all business is carried on by spoken agreement. The bond that one gives in spoken assent becomes one's most important accreditation.

If, however, no objections lie, the almost inaudible tones of the Speaker flow over the clerk's reading like a benediction. "The bill is ordered engrossed and read for a third time, prior two readings dispensed with, there being no objection. The bill is agreed to. A motion to reconsider is laid on the table." The formal ritual words are spoken, and the House has acted. A bill has been enacted. There may be only fifteen Members on the Floor at the time, but all the protective devices of a great governing body have locked in place, while the forms and ritual are satisfied.

The Speaker, through whom all of this consent must be filtered, is immediately and continuously available. As he leaves the dais, he will be stopped in the Speaker's Lobby by four or five persons. He stands stolid and square, clamping down hard on a cigarette with his teeth, then rolling it along between his lips. Or he may sit on one of the overstuffed mohair couches beaming and smiling, giving a nod to everyone who may pass by.

The Speaker's Lobby is a long corridor running the length of the Chamber behind the Speaker's dais. Only congressmen and certain newspaper correspondents are permitted use of this hallway. Leading off the Lobby are several converted reading rooms which have the unhappy air of railroad waiting rooms—airless, dingy and bare.

Across the hall, the Speaker has his offices. His own personal office seems about half the size of a railroad car, and reminds one, inescapably, of an old-fashioned parlor car. There is the red carpeting, clean and antiseptic. Resplendent cutglass light fixtures. The creamy ochre walls of public buildings. A few ashtrays featuring reproductions of the Capitol dome. No books. No papers. No pictures to speak of or remember. The ascetic trappings of this man's public life, stripped for action, not for contemplation or remembrance.

This is where the endless delegations come to tell the Speaker their stories. An appointment is arranged by telephone. Singly, in twos or threes or more, the Speaker will see us all when we feel the need. A matter of national significance, a matter of personality, a matter of individual trouble—the Speaker listens, friendly and attentively. He has heard it so many times. But this attention is riveted out of deference to the close-knit feeling for the House and its Members, great and small. Attentiveness, a precious political commodity because of its rarity, is one means he employs to cement the bonds. For the Speaker is not only the outward and visible symbol of the House, but he is its inward guardian and counsellor.

Very sincerely,

Clem Miller

Dear Friend:

The "Leadership," that loose collection of advisors and confidants surrounding the Speaker of the House, prefers to observe the proper channels of legislative process because it is the most dependable route to legislative success. This method minimizes defeat that would surely erode its power. The Leadership is very sensitive to those massive forces that build and build behind legislation for years. It knows to a hair when to yield before such pressure, and loose the floodgates of power. Such a climax is building on the Wilderness Bill, for example. And School Support. And perhaps the Area Redevelopment Bill.

Every once in a while, however, something happens to the process of judgment, and the consensus of rank-and-file opinion gets at crosscurrent with the Leadership. Such a situation is apparently now developing over certain proposals to lift the interest rate ceiling on long-term United States bonds.

Low interest rates and fears of "Wall Street" go to the very core of Democratic party philosophy. This was demonstrated last year when the Simpson Amendment on raising the interest rate was opposed by a solid Democratic vote (except for one defector).

Somehow or other, the Leadership has become convinced that raising the ceiling is a good idea. Leaving party philosophy out of it, the Speaker has even been convinced that it is good medicine politically. The Speaker felt strongly enough to go in person to the Democrats on the Ways and Means Committee and to throw his tremendous prestige behind a "compromise" bill to raise the ceiling. With his stirring and prodding, Democrats went in favor, 8 to 7. Republicans, of course, were solid, and the bill was sent to Rules.

Because of this fundamental disagreement over a traditional Democratic policy, sentiment is shaping up for a party caucus. A caucus can be called by the Leadership. (Only two have been called since World War II.) A caucus can also be set in motion by a petition signed by fifty Members. If a caucus should convene, and if two-thirds vote in favor of any position, it then becomes binding for the entire party. (Members may be excused under certain conditions.)

It is fascinating to follow the reasoning for and against a caucus call. First, a caucus would bring out into the open opposition to the Leadership. There are those who think this is desirable, purely as salutary admonition—that a show of force will result in more consideration for the "back-benchers." Others contend that a show of force without victory or substantial strength will result in no change or in even greater autocracy.

The question then is, Do we have the strength for a meaningful show of force? It boils down to an evaluation. Is the interest rate issue sufficiently strong to pull the waverers from the shirttails of the Leadership? Many who would otherwise hold to the traditional Democratic view will support the Leadership as a matter of party organization. Southern votes which we might get on the Floor of the House as a matter of tradition, principle, and conviction, we would lose in a caucus vote because the threat to the Leadership is more explicit than the party philosophy.

The dilemma remains, however: How can the overwhelming sentiment of the rank-and-file Democrats be transmitted to the Leadership without constituting a threat to its power? How can discussion of an issue take place without an implied challenge?

Among the newer Members there is restiveness. There is the desire to be heard. Yet, there is awareness of responsibility. Most Members realize that Leadership must retain the reins of party organization if it is to lead in other battles. Many do not believe that a party caucus constitutes a threat to the Leadership; they feel it may actually strengthen it. These Members believe that there is a need for more reciprocity and exchange between the Leadership and the rank and file so that feelings will not grow so high that a challenge to the Leadership finally becomes inevitable. In the past, such matters have been resolved by private negotiation and accommodation. Heat and steam are dissipated in the system: 1) through the filing of minority views within committee, and 2) in debate on the Floor. Through these convenient devices an issue is diverted to one of general principle rather than of party faith. Threats to party structure are sort of homogenized.

Since the Leadership is firmly in the saddle both in committee and on the Floor, this dissent on general principle becomes empty vaporing, having little more effect than the strength which lent it breath.

Again using the interest rate dispute as an example, it was suggested to the acting Speaker that it should appropriately be taken to a caucus as a matter of individual conscience, which could then be debated on the Floor on its merits. He seeks to avoid a caucus discussion which might lead to overt challenge to the Leadership. Thus, the Leadership seeks to avoid a preliminary skirmish that might eventually result in a great showdown between the North and the South—the spectre behind the prospect of any Democratic party caucus or meeting.

Very sincerely,

Clem Miller

Dear Friend:

The House of Representatives is organized by the Majority party, and the Majority party in its organizational meetings during the opening week of each Congress (every two years), hands over its powers to the Leadership.

The Leadership is the Speaker and whoever else he may consent to counsel with. Currently this includes the Majority Leader, the Majority Whip, a few committee chairmen, and others.

The Speaker seeks to make his rulership as benign as possible. He will see any Democrat upon any provocation. Delegations wait upon him, or individuals—and promptly, with dispatch he says, "Certainly, Mr. ——, tomorrow at nine?"

Groups cluster in the big antechamber outside his "official" office just off the Floor of the House. Six or eight of us crowd about, ushered into the half of a railway car by his quite correct and unassuming aide. The Speaker is very friendly. The mouth, so down-curved for public ceremony, turns up readily and warmly in private. We range ourselves on the edges of chairs and sofas. The conversation begins all brisk and rapid-fire, about this and that and the other. The Speaker answers easily, and in good humor. His eye flicks over the group. He is a coachman for a poorly harnessed team. When will we begin? As I am the only freshman, he singles me out for special comment. This is simply delightful. Finally, a senior member of the group says, "Now, Mr. Speaker, about the Depressed Areas Bill."

The joviality evaporates. But just as easily as before, the Speaker responds, "When are you boys going to do something about them upstairs?" He gestures towards the ceiling, above which the Rules Committee has its rooms.

"That's what we came to see *you* about." The Speaker tries another tack. "With everything going well in the country . . . this bill . . . I don't see any great need for it." At once a chorus of anguish. We are ready for him on this. In rapid salvos everyone present, each experienced in the science of telling words, fires off bits—his reasons why this bill is needed now. There is even a scattering of shot—about aircraft shutdowns in Texas. We had received reports of the Speaker's doubts about the urgency of this bill, and to be forewarned is to be forearmed. So many problems of Congress are of such long standing that, many times, the basic issues get clouded with the passage of time. Everyone had presumed that the Speaker knew the facts about the depressed areas legislation. He had heard the story retold over so many years. Actually, his information was out-of-date.

'Round the room we went, each adding a fast reappraisal of the need for this legislation.

The Speaker saw this was no group to go through the center with, so he tried his first move again. When were we going to do something with the Democratic members of the Rules Committee? And what could we do, we asked? We were asking the help of the Speaker with the gentlemen upstairs. The ball remained in midfield. The interview limped to a close.

Had there been achievement? Perhaps. Perhaps a fresh understanding by the Speaker of a perplexing national disgrace. Perhaps a word would go out "upstairs." Perhaps he would not put in a fatal objection should we try something on our own. The question, as always, boiled down to an appraisal—did we have the votes? Yes, the Speaker was interested in the currency of the problem itself. He was interested in the connection between chronically depressed areas and the areas of automation and technological change. But—but, he asked, could we produce the needed votes when and if we got to the Floor?

To this, we had chorused assent. Yes, we had the votes by a wide margin if we could only go to a test.

And right here is raised the dilemma of the Leadership. Yes, they lead, but they lead only because they win. If they cannot be certain of winning, they don't want to go. Latent power, negative power, is so much better than power committed that lacks victory as a capstone. Hence, the legislative timidity of the Congress, both House and Senate. Hence, the timidity is compounded in the face of a threatened veto, when one-third of either Chamber becomes the majority in a very real sense. Hence, the great time lags for the consideration of legislation, stretching into years in many cases, while the Leadership waits for the pressures to build—pressures that will produce success. Hence, the aversion of the Leadership for impatience, for intemperate haste. Hence, the distaste for short cuts that may bring legislation out of committee prematurely without sufficient regard for victory; distaste for battle just for the sake of the battle, distaste for the Discharge Petition, and for Calendar Wednesday, and for the Democratic Caucus. Righteousness with victory is a fine thing. Righteousness with defeat is nothing much at all.

Very sincerely,

Clem Miller

Dear Friend:

One's overwhelming first impression as a Member of Congress is the aura of friendliness that surrounds the life of a congressman. No wonder that "few die and none resign." Almost everyone is unfailingly polite and courteous. Window washers, clerks, senators —it cuts all ways.

We live in a cocoon of good feeling—no doubt the compensation for the cruel political buffeting that is received in the world outside. And we can immediately appreciate how Congress or the congressman can shield it or himself from reality, losing touch with the facts of life if not watchful.

The freshman congressman is being constantly made aware of the necessity, even the imperative, of getting along with his fellow congressmen. Congress is a large body. To accomplish anything, the procedure must be formalized—obeisance must be paid to tradition, to seniority.

We are constantly being reminded of this fact by our elders. Briefings by liberal and conservative alike are filled with admonitions to attend to the niceties and necessities of precedence. But the very practical requirement to get along with your fellow legislator may clash with the overriding need for political drama in the world outside.

As Max Freedman in the *Guardian* has pointed out, the battle over the filibuster is regarded in the Senate as a procedural affair to enable that body to conduct its business. To the country at large, however, it is a drama of civil rights. The failure of the Senate to dramatize this basic struggle has been greeted around the country with deep dismay.

To a lesser extent, a similar battle has been waged in the House over a proposed "twenty-one day rule." This rule would say simply that a bill referred to the Rules Committee might be discharged for a vote of the House in twenty-one days. Presumably, this would prevent the very conservative Rules Committee from bottling up legislation. (Actually, it is doubtful if Congress would employ the twenty-one day rule even if it were a part of the procedure. Tradition would stand in the way.)

Prior to the convening of Congress a representative of the liberal bloc in the House conferred with Speaker Rayburn. The Speaker assured him that any legislation, properly submitted to the Rules Committee, would be brought to the Floor for a vote. This pledge was acceptable to the group as being more valuable than a fight for the issue on the Floor. It was a hard decision to make. The value of dramatizing the issue for the country was realized. And it was not simply that we would be beaten, though we would have been. At most we had 120-50 votes out of 436. The 80 votes of last year have undoubtedly been augmented by the newcomers. There are 78 of us. But to expect that we would be able to charge into the fray the opening day has no more possibility of success than any green troops if put to battle after marching all night. The associations which might lead to confident action simply do not exist.

To understand the agreement one must appreciate the tremendous respect for Speaker Rayburn in all ranks. This veneration is very deep and has many compounds. It is an extremely powerful elixir. Thus, we might say that we are staking our faith in Mr. Rayburn's prestige against the effects which a Floor fight might have had. Since one would be appealing in the first instance to his fellow congressmen, and in the latter instance to the country, it was a hard choice to make.

Only time will tell whether it was a good choice. In the meantime, to those sitting in the gallery on opening day, it was a casual matter. An elderly gentleman with long hair curling over his ears —Howard Smith of Virginia (long-time Chairman of the Rules Committee)—getting to his feet . . . "Mr. Speaker, I offer a Resolution . . . that the rules of the 85th Congress be adopted as the Rules of the 86th Congress." The Speaker hardly glances up. The swell of conversation barely abates. A few strangled "ayes," a "nay" or two. "So ordered." The rules have not been changed.

Very sincerely,

Clem Miller

CHAPTER III

POWER

THE WORD "power" has been defined in many ways. It may refer to the strength which a nation has in influencing or controlling other nations. If one speaks of individual power, he may mean the ability to control or to influence others either by physical force, craft, or leadership. In the sense that the term power is used with reference to Congress, the definition "ability to do or act; capability of doing or effecting something" applies. A person who has power in Congress is someone who can get things done or who can keep things from being done if he so desires. It is obvious that no person has complete power. Congress is not a rubber stamp for an individual or even a small group of individuals. But there are powerful congressmen, and there are congressmen who are almost totally ineffective. There are always leaders, men of power, natural leaders in any group. Most of the Members of Congress are or have been leaders; if this were not so they never would have been elected. Why then do some congressmen have power and others seem to get nowhere despite their heroic efforts?

Power does not come necessarily from party regularity. Many powerful people constantly disagree with other powerful people of the same party. Wilson said, "Power is nowhere concentrated; it is rather deliberately and of set policy scattered amongst many small chiefs."[1] This is a way of defining power in terms of the mechanics of organization. The two loose confederations in the House which we call political parties organize the House. The leader of the majority party becomes the Speaker. Committee assignments are made on the basis of seniority in the House. The freshmen start out on an equal footing, with some getting more desirable assign-

[1] Woodrow Wilson, *op. cit.*, p. 92.

ments than others. Rankings within a committee are based on seniority in that particular committee, and the chairman and a majority of the members are from the majority party in the House. Seniority is the key to assignment and, as such, is the key to tremendous power.

Power is personal as well as hierarchical. It springs from the rules and precedents mentioned in the last chapter. It may come to some outside the upper levels of the hierarchy. It never comes to a freshman!

The following letters give a glimpse of how power functions in the House—how things are done, how changes are effected.

Dear Friend:

Last week in the House of Representatives a southern freshman addressed the Members in his maiden remarks. In part, this is what he said: ". . . there is definite evidence that subversive activities are at the base or at the root of our school problems in the South."

The story of how this gentleman came to attain his seat in the face of grave and troublesome election irregularities may be set forth as a compound of precedent, procedure, maneuver, and power. Many of us were disarmed at the start by an agreement that he should stand aside while everyone else was sworn in. (He was then sworn in at a separate ceremony pending investigation of his status.) We were further beguiled by the rumor which was spread through the halls that he would be seated, but not as a Democrat. The fact is that he will take his seat after exhaustive hearings, and he now is listed in the directories as a Democrat.

How does this happen? Why doesn't the substantial majority which would oppose seating this man register protests? First, there is the hard certainty that he would be overwhelmingly re-elected if we should refuse to seat him. The futility of such a gesture is a depressant to action. Second, there is precedent, that most powerful of House levers. And precedents are against us in this case. We have seated all kinds of men in the past—men guilty of fraud, felony, and every kind of irregularity. These factors weighed heavily in this case.

And finally there are the procedures of the House which work for the man. One must comprehend that all House action springs from one committee or another. It is by means of the committee process that the 435 Members of the House are held to some semblance of order, and that the work of Congress is organized and put through. This monolithic, glacial action is refined to an even finer tolerance by our committee chairmen. In this particular case, we felt an issue should be made of party affiliation. The question is how party responsibility can be built if office holders drift in and out of their party at will. And on this point, we were told that the man's committee appointment would be taken out of the Republican committee quota and that he would be seated as an Independent. Then, when nothing could be done about it, the Committee on Committees reported out the full list of committee assignments. The new man was at the very bottom, but carried as a Democrat. When the matter came to the Floor, as a committee matter, backed up by the tremendous prestige of its chairman, one would have had to vote against himself in order to vote against the report. It came before Congress in its entirety. The opposition had been neatly fragmented into seventy-eight pieces. The matter was closed.

It is probably difficult for those of you at home to understand how this apparently placid maneuver could take place. It is not difficult to see from here. As newcomers, without organization, without the sense of trust and interdependence that comes from long association, we lack any locus of power. The interior lines of communication and strength are contained in the hands of those who have been here for many years. The organization and procedures of the House make it well-nigh impossible to speak out as an individual. And it is unwise to speak out as a group unless (a) you have the votes to win, or (b) you have a really grand canvas upon which to spread a public protest. The progressive leaders felt that this case did not present the scope for such a protest. A big price must be paid for defeat. When you pay that price, the resulting public achievement must be worth it.

But the gentleman in question has put the South on the spot as well as the nation, and a lot of southern congressmen are privately unhappy. Every district has an extremist who can outshout any incumbent. One congressman confided that such a person in his district could beat him. He said, "I believe in law and order. When it comes to defying the law, I've got to step aside. I've got to fight for our laws." This congressman would be an easy mark for a demagogue.

Very sincerely,

Clem Miller

Dear Friend:

I have been trying to describe and delineate the troubles and problems of political leadership as well as those of party responsibility in the House. There are similar problems in the Senate. Here, in my mind, is an excellent insight which I hope you will find interesting. It was in the February 5th "Congressional Report" of the National Committee for an Effective Congress:[2]

On January 12, 1960, meeting in closed session, the Democratic members of the Senate voted 51-12 to defeat a motion by Albert Gore of Tennessee, and 51-11 to pass a motion by Mike Mansfield of Montana.

These results were conveyed immediately to fifty-odd newspaper and broadcasting people camped in the corridor outside, and a few minutes later were trumpeted to the nation as another stunning defeat for the "liberals."

The general public was given an impression—doubly false, but strangely satisfying to the die-hards on both sides—that the "liberals" have less than a third of the strength they normally muster on substantive issues, and that Johnson is a kind of Congressional Carmine de Sapio riding roughshod over all opposition.

So ended what the *Washington Post* casually dismissed as the liberals' "annual uprising" against the leadership. What really happened, and how significant was it? . . . When William Proxmire called last year for "regular caucuses (on) our legislative program," he was seeking to reverse a leadership situation that had developed without design over half a century. Fifty years ago, the Senate Democratic caucus, or conference, was a powerful instrument. A vote of two-thirds of its members was binding upon each individual Senator and determined his vote on the floor. This system broke down after World War I, following the passage of the 17th amendment, which provided for direct election of Senators. As long as Senators had been elected by state legislatures, they could afford to make the deals implicit in accepting the discipline of the caucus; once they had to justify themselves to the people, they could no longer accept that discipline. The system was almost completely eroded during the Roosevelt and Truman administrations, when legislative recommendations flowed from the White House and the task of the Democratic leadership was merely to see that they were processed as smoothly as possible.

[2] This article originally appeared in the *St. Louis Post-Dispatch* and is reprinted here with their permission.

Recently, virtually the only function of the Senate Democratic conference has been to elect the party's floor leader; and under Lyndon Johnson, conference meetings had been limited to one each year.

That this lack of conference activity could have lasted six years for a party without a President and as variously represented as the Democrats are in the Senate, is a tribute to Johnson's skill as a leader—to the perceptiveness with which he determined the consensus and the fidelity with which he represented it. . . .

There has always been a tendency among some to blame Johnson for what were, in fact, errors of the consensus. But now the situation has changed substantially. Now, even many of Johnson's more tolerant colleagues complain that he no longer represents the consensus; and that frequently he deliberately ignores it.

Several factors have helped to produce this change:

1) The balance of power within the Democratic Party in the Senate has shifted greatly as a result of the election in 1958 of large numbers of new Democrats from northern and western states. It is no longer so easy to play the two extremes against each other and come up on dead center.

2) The size of the Democratic majority tends to weaken discipline. The threat of a defection is not so frightening when it does not raise the possibility of Republicans taking over.

3) Scenting a possibility of winning the presidency for the first time in eight years, the northern and western members are less inclined to be patient with a "stand pat" policy of bipartisan cooperation with the administration. . . .

Against this background, the real result of the meetings of the Democratic conference early this month was quite different from what was reported to the public.

The principal objective of the liberals was to secure additional meetings of the conference for discussion of substantive legislative issues. Senator Clark (Pa.) had prepared a resolution providing for such meetings to be held at the request of fifteen Senators, and it was expected that a fight would develop around this motion. However, as soon as the issue was raised at the meeting on January 7, Johnson said that he had "promised" in 1953 that a meeting would be called whenever requested by any individual Senator, and that the promise was still good.

This commitment was so sweeping that it aroused a degree of concern among some members as to the possibility that meetings might be called too lightly, and at the instance of colleagues seeking only personal publicity rather than serious attention to an issue. However, after some discussion, a consensus was reached as to calling meetings of the conference whenever one was seriously desired, and it was accepted without a vote that such a decision had been made and will be implemented. . . .

Only after this very substantial victory did there begin the maneuvers which got the play in the press and gave the appearance of a disastrous liberal defeat.

As described by *Senator A* (who voted *with Johnson*), Johnson took exception to some of the remarks that had been made during the discussion on conference meetings. He felt they reflected on his leadership, and made the "bad mistake" of getting angry. He called attention to the honored membership of the Policy Committee and implied that any criticism of him must also be taken as criticism of them. The Policy Committee does not, in fact, set policy. It merely determines the timing of the legislative schedule—and no one has had any complaint against it. But Johnson's anger so aroused some of the liberals that they immediately vowed to "do something" about the Policy Committee.

Another meeting was held on January 12, and the Gore Resolution was not introduced until then. This resolution called for the enlargement of the Policy Committee, for its members to be elected by the conference rather than appointed by Johnson, and for the Committee to attempt to work out legislative policy lines for the Senate Democrats.

According to *Senator B* (who voted *against Johnson*), the issue posed by the Policy Committee resolution introduced by Senator Gore was not advantageously framed and little or no effort was made to enlist supporters for it. Both these facts contributed to, if they did not dictate, its defeat by a vote of 51-12. "It injected an entirely new issue which even we who voted with Gore had not thought through," the Senator said.

After more than two hours of discussion of the Gore resolution, and after it was voted down, Carroll (Colo.) rose to suggest that some thought be given to the possibility of electing members of the Steering Committee in the future. (This group makes the committee assignments which are the basis of senatorial careers. Its members presently are appointed by the leader.) Although Carroll had not made a motion, and merely suggested that thought be given to the idea, Johnson sensed an opportunity for another victory. Mansfield (Montana), the party whip, moved for a vote against changing the procedure for selection of Steering Committee members—and this carried by 51-11. Senator B thought this vote "involved a clear matter of principle, and many more of our friends should have been with us."

Senator C (who voted *with Johnson*) claims that no one seriously wanted the reforms which were rejected in these two votes. "The motions were made just to embarrass Johnson's presidential hopes," he said. "I voted against them for two reasons. First, however I may disagree with him sometimes, I think he has been a good enough leader not to deserve that kind of treatment from us. Second, we have other presidential candidates here, and we're not going to accomplish anything during this session if we all start playing this way."

Senator D (who voted *against Johnson*) said that the issue was whether the Democrats could begin to have a party position and project a party image. Having the Policy Committee try to chart party policy in the Senate might not work out, he said, "but we should at least experiment with it." Finding a successful formula by which Policy Committee drafts of positions would be amended or ratified by the conference at the beginning of each session "would enable the public to know whenever any Democrat votes like a Republican. There's too much of that going undetected now."

Senator E (who voted *with Johnson*) said even his liberal colleagues are too concerned with protecting the interest groups in their own states to be bound by either the Policy Committee or the conference. "I'd vote for it if they were willing to be bound," he declared, "but when Frear (Del.) pointed to each of them and asked if they would be bound they each said 'no.' What sense does that make? Also, I see no point in the meetings. We all know what the others think. The fellows who do all the talking on the floor (of the Senate) are the same ones who would do the talking at meetings. I'm too busy as things are to listen to any more. What would make some sense would be a liberal conference. The liberals in the House have a smart, well-organized and effective operation going (the Democratic Study Group, headed by Lee Metcalf of Montana). If the fellows on the same side here would try to work together, I'd be for that. But there are too many prima donnas here."

A final word was added by a *top Senate staff member* whose feelings toward the Leadership are such that he probably would have voted with the liberals had he been a Senator, but who would have had no confidence in that vote. "An elected Policy Committee would probably be worse than what Johnson has appointed," he said. "Under the seniority system, the senior members exert such influence over the votes of the junior members that they would effectively control the selection of the Policy Committee," he pointed out. "All Senators are equal, but some Senators are more equal than others, and Lyndon Johnson is the most equal. Fortunately," he concluded, "Johnson hasn't done badly by the liberals in making their own committee appointments, and in selecting the members of the Policy and Steering Committees."

The real and for the most part unreported significance of all this is revealed in the fact that a meeting of the Democratic conference was held the following week to discuss the education bill—the first meeting on a substantive issue since 1952. About half of the Democratic Senators attended and there was a spirited and genial discussion of the pending bill for federal aid for school construction. Senator Clark made a strong statement on behalf of his amendment for federal aid for teachers' salaries, and picked up sufficient support to introduce the amendment with twenty-two sponsors.

Although the leadership was present at this meeting, it was significant that most of the opponents of the bill did not attend. As a result, no differences of opinion were threshed out and no attempt was made to record a consensus. However, the meeting revealed, to those most interested in the bill, the extent of the support they could count on, and it provided an opportunity for discussion they might not otherwise have had. In this respect, it was worthwhile. Since additional meetings are expected to be held on other issues, a further evaluation of the significance of the "uprising" must await their results.

Very sincerely,

Clem Miller

Dear Friend:

Today I wish to return to the individual and his relation to power. An analogy with medieval warfare is suggested here. The congressman may seek to take the castle by scaling the walls in open combat or by a sapping operation under the moat. Scaling the walls means making many Floor speeches, getting in on every debate from railroad pensions to the color of oranges, putting on the hair shirt for the public and the press, etc. The structure of Congress consigns this course to almost certain failure. The very qualities of public show, of defiance, of bravery, are looked at askance. The congressman who speaks constantly, even if cogently, cannot seem to acquire respect. Even his friends begin to avoid him.

On the other hand, the congressman who consults privately with shrewdness, who has just come from a closed meeting with somebody with information to impart, who works quietly underground, will wind up in the donjon with the prize. He will, in the course of time, exert influence. He will be asked for his opinion. In a profession which makes much of handing out advice, it is being asked for it that is the greatest jewel.

People speculate and newspapermen occasionally complain about why the congressman doesn't speak out. He doesn't speak out because this is not the way to power. Power is in silence, in committee, in personal relations. If a frustrated congressman must speak out, he can do so in the Appendix of the *Congressional Record*. (This fascinating department furnishes the complete outlet for congressional feelings. Contents are limited only by the discretion of the individual.) If the congressman actually wishes to exercise his vocal chords as part of his therapy, he can talk to an empty House at the close of the regular business under another curious institution called "Special Orders."

There is another reason why speaking out in the House is not favored. It is because such public display is largely fruitless. The fact is that no one reports congressional debate.

The idea of the House as a forum for public expression is a huge fiction which should be recognized. Debate in the House is usually a shallow thing, difficult to follow, and it must be very difficult to report. Therefore, the press pays almost no attention to debate in the House. Reporters are where power is. They don't waste their valuable time in the House press gallery unless an important vote is to be taken. They are to be found in the Speaker's Lobby where the powerful are.

As I have indicated, reputations are seldom made in debate. But reputations can be lost by seeking the public way to power—in the open assault over the walls. Some congressmen are known as the "kiss of death" because their public display drives off votes. In one lively exchange, an urbane New Yorker asked a certain congressman to yield, and asked, "You are for my bill?" When the answer came in the affirmative, the New Yorker hurried up the aisle, his arms waving over his head in mock horror, symbolizing certain defeat. He lost, too.

It is a matter of the greatest interest how reputations are hung on a man. It goes to the nature of Congress, I suppose. The political relationship is at one and the same time intensely personal, and yet blandly impersonal. The typical congressman exudes personal friendship by the yard. Everyone is a bosom buddy from the word go—first names all over the place, affectionate grabs of arms and shoulders, pats and taps. A sick Member returning is the center of warm attention. Praise is bandied around in wholesale lots, and your first trips to this candy factory leave you feeling a little heavy.

Yet, this intense, clubby, personal relationship continually smacks with great force directly into the cold, cruel hardness of the vote. The close friend you were grimacing with not two minutes before votes with the other people. You may be able to shrug this off by rationalizing that "he's voting his district," but frequently it hurts. On certain key votes this effect is monstrous to such a degree that new alignments, stock-taking, etc., occur. "It's not only his neck," you speculate. "He's putting his/my party on the block. He's putting *me* on the block."

This alternation between the role of buddy and executioner, in greater or lesser degree, creates great strains that often become almost intolerable. That politicians have thick skins is simply not a reliable opinion. Politicians are usually in politics because they are "feeling" people. Their feelings toward one another are the most acute of all. Hence, a session of Congress is a wearing affair.

The result of these sharp-honed feelings is an enlarged apperception that is used to scrutinize fellow Members. While congressmen are quite ordinary in general outline, their practice of the political art has made them knowledgeable in assessing one another. Their instincts, sharpened by this conflict of the personal and the impersonal, enable them to characterize each other to the finest hair. Thus, each congressman is given his own little pigeonhole, with all his strengths and weaknesses, foibles and tricks, duly noted for use on the proper occasions. Power, then, is the respect which accrues and adheres to those individuals who are best able to stand this daily etching process.

Very sincerely,

Clem Miller

Dear Friend:

In recent weeks we have been talking about the locus of congressional power. Let us now relate it to the Floor of the House. Previously, we have seen that as an issue mounts in importance, ability to influence on the Floor of the House lessens.

We have also seen that debate changes few votes. Now let us consider how votes *are* changed. Members do change the votes of other Members and Members do switch from vote to vote. This is done on a personal basis. But shifts of this kind seldom change a final result. Final results are almost always changed only by a hierarchic shift. Even in these instances, substantial hierarchic changes can be made without immediately altering the final result. For example, the South is shifting from a pro-mutual security position to one opposed. There was a shift of thirty-four votes between 1958 and 1959. However, the influx of northern Democrats cancelled the effect this shift might otherwise have had.

Now, to understand the manner in which an individual might be induced to change his vote, let us first examine the seating arrangements in the House Chamber. Republicans arrange themselves on the Speaker's left, Democrats on his right. Attendance is a chancy affair. Democrats outnumber Republicans generally, but the latter are there when they have to be.

There are no assigned seats in the Chamber. There are characteristic groupings. Illinois always sits in a back corner. Massachusetts has a steady little knot in the center aisle. The southerners arrange themselves in a boot-shaped group behind the majority tables. Kentucky is a solid row, center aisle. And immediately behind them sit Brock and McGinley of Nebraska in what you might call the left-field bleachers. Connecticut sits together but the place changes from day to day. I could go blindfolded to the seats many Members habitually sit in. Others stand behind the rail, in the rear. Others stand along the sides, and never sit at all. Others walk in one door to respond to their names at roll calls and immediately exit by another. Others inhabit the cloakroom.

Then there are the floaters, going from group to group, taking soundings, reporting rumors. "How are you going to vote on the ————Bill?" The floaters link the sub-blocs to establish a consensus.

Let's see how this works out in practice. Let us refer to a bill relatively devoid of party overtones—for example, the Auto Safety Bill. Some representatives seemed to be against it because it might cost some money in the Department of Commerce. Other congressmen were for it because it promised to save lives, and thus, they argued, would save money in the long run. But by and large, there was doubt and hesitation. Everywhere the call was, "How are you going to vote?" State delegations sent representatives around to do private polling. No one appeared to be following the debate. There was banter back and forth. "Are you against *saving lives?*" "What are you, a *spender?*" Little knots of conversation, much of it seeming idle or irrelevant, actually signified a working out of opinions. The roll begins: "Abbitt, Abernathy, Adair, Addonizio. . . ." Some wait for bellwethers. They pass over the first call, listening for key votes.

I saw one influential Democrat listening to a friend who wants him to vote "no." He does so. Then, later, he taps another friend on the shoulder. "How'd you vote?" The other friend voted for it. Sheepishly, and amidst some kidding, "influential" gets up at the call's end to change his vote. A small incident, but this is the working out of power. "Another friend" has power because he was consulted by one with power.

The most interesting roll call of the session, in my mind, was on the so-called Vault Cash Bill. This was designed, among other things, to lower reserves of Federal Reserve member banks. It was regarded as a giveaway of billions by some. To others, it constituted a small but significant addition to inflation. To most, it was a confusing bill, almost incomprehensible and not very significant.

Some Members asked friends, "Is it a giveaway?" "No, but . . ." The floaters scurried back and forth. At the end, in frustrated confusion, many Members went with the committee chairman who had reported the bill favorably. The fact that it gave advantages to banks stirred the embers of the old Populist sentiment and fanned the sparks of a younger group. These congressmen were aroused and they were convinced on a personal basis. The leadership of the committee chairman was not persuasive to them. However, the tradition of following the chairman was strong enough to hold a majority to his side, so the revolt failed.

What may be learned from these examples is that voting lines are set by the committee chairmen (and by each committee's senior minority member) and hence by the Leadership; that generally this is sufficient to carry the day; and finally, that individuals may shift back and forth within this framework in response to personal appeals and deeply ingrained prejudices. The total effect is a series of decisions inspired by committee leaders, but lacking coordinated, overall policy direction.

Very sincerely,

Clem Miller

Dear Friend:

This is basically a report on power in the House of Representatives. It must be tentative, as all such things are.

As I see it, power in the House is a personal thing. A congressman accedes to power by his own personal actions over a period of time. Having said that, let me quickly contradict myself by saying that power is also hierarchical in nature. Power adheres to committee chairmen, and filters slowly down to the lower ranks.

As I have reported previously, Congress is a collection of committees that come together in a Chamber periodically to approve one another's actions. The committee chairman or ranking minority member becomes the rallying point for his party in any debate on any given bill. Unlike other deliberative bodies, the Floor Leader for a piece of legislation is the committee chairman rather than the Majority Leader.

Members will frequently, and even customarily, follow a committee chairman against their own best interests and against the dictates of friendship or reason. A case comes vividly to mind. On the Landrum-Griffin Bill the chairman of the committee had agreed with the Republicans to sacrifice what seemed to him a good amendment in order to get their approval on the overall bill, thus forestalling a bitter battle. A minority of us on the committee made a vigorous Floor fight on this amendment which we also regarded as desirable. The facts, the presentation, and the merits were all on the side of a "yes" vote. Yet, on a standing vote, a good share of the Democrats stood up with the chairman to say "nay," although we felt no case had been made.

Such loyalty to committee chairmen may undergo revision in our next session. When the Landrum-Griffin Bill was up for vote, thirteen of the nineteen committee chairmen deserted the Speaker to favor the bill. This graphically illustrated the locus of power in the House. The Speaker, unable to deliver votes, was revealed in outline against the chairmen. This fact was not lost on Democratic Members. Last January the Speaker pledged that legislation would not be permitted to languish in committee or to be forestalled by the Rules Committee. The Landrum-Griffin Bill was mute evidence that this pledge could not be redeemed. Those who (with excellent hindsight) now criticize the agreement with the Speaker should be reminded that until the redemption of this pledge was made clear to all, no one could make a move.

The effect of this new appraisal may be detected in several un-noted votes after this time. For example, the Chairman of the Agriculture Committee opposed an amendment to an agricultural bill offered by a ranking Republican. He glanced around at the substantial Democratic membership arrayed behind him, but was dismayed to see seventy of them stand up with the Republican's forces to carry the amendment against the southern Democrats, 153-52.

Another interesting series of votes occurred on the second housing bill. The Republicans proposed a series of limiting amendments. The southerners bounced up about forty strong to vote with the Republicans for the first amendment on a teller, pass-through count. The hostility on the part of other Democrats to this action was as visible as an unsheathed knife. Then, as each amendment came along fewer southerners arose with the Republicans, till at last there were only five left, conspicuously self-conscious.

If these are portents for the next session, and well they might be, chairmen will not be so successful in securing the automatic allegiance of their junior colleagues. This could mean some shift of power.

It is more likely, however, that any coalition of northern forces will have only limited success. Congressional government, by the design of our forefathers, does not encourage coordinate political action. A coalition of northerners, without interior lines of strength, is a tenuous thing. The very reason many are here is that they tend to be individualistic, hence not readily amenable to central authority. There is no unifying philosophy such as the issue of segregation is to the southerners. While northern Democrats have generally similar objectives, on any given vote there is enough disagreement among them to result in noticeable defection and frequent defeat.

Let us return to the analogy with warfare. The committees with their chairmen are like a string of forts. The northern coalition, as the attackers, are spread out, with poor communication and hence poor coordination. They have no base of power from which to menace the chairmen on the one hand, or to discipline their members on the other.

The greatest hazard to the besiegers, however, is the undependability of their coalition. They may have determined a strategy, only to discover that one of the barons has left the line with his levies to return home, or to sue for a separate peace with the defenders. Certain significant blocs of votes owe their primary and definitive allegiance to their city or state, and the outlines of broad policy always give way before local needs.

A graphic example comes to mind. On the vote to override Eisenhower's second public works veto, one leader who controlled four other votes on this issue held those votes out till the end. The vote was very close. We could all see him negotiating about something with the Majority Leader near the Speaker's rostrum. Finally, the bloc's votes were recorded in favor of the override. The results of the negotiations are not known to me. Perhaps it was a tour de force. But the lesson was there. If a leader were willing to jeopardize his party on such a major test of strength, it is not hard to see how much more this is true in lesser but still significant matters.

Very sincerely,

Clem Miller

Dear Friend:

This is the legislative time of year for the "conference" committee, the "conference" report, and thus, the season for final passage of the bills which have been in process since the opening days of the session. The conference is the little-known device by which differences between the House version of a bill and its Senate counterpart are worked out. Each body, House and Senate, appoints conferees. There may be four or eight or nine, with representation from the Republican and Democratic sides, proportioned to their relative strength in the whole membership.

Conference committees make their own rules. The watchword is informality. Committee meetings are bargaining sessions between principals who know the game. The preliminaries are out of the way. Now is the time to hammer out the finished product.

Presumably the conference has the duty of resolving, by compromise, the differences between House and Senate. If all goes well, this is achieved. The resultant bill, identical to the last comma, is returned to each house. No amendment is possible, accept or reject. Almost always the conference report is adopted. If things do not go so well, and agreement seems impossible, conferees return to their respective houses to ask for "instructions." At the same time, the conferees "suggest" that we recede on this point, stand fast there, agree on another. Our concurrence is readily had. Armed with these "instructions," the conferees return to the battle until all-encompassing agreement is reached. Should no agreement be possible, the bill is dead.

In actual practice, the conference report is far more than a compromise between the houses. Very frequently it is a goal, a haven for legislative policy. It is a rare House chairman who pilots his bill through the House without keeping at least one eye on the conference which will almost certainly result, for rarely does an important bill exactly conform to the companion bill in the Senate. When he so affably makes points with a Member by adopting his pet amendment, the chairman knows he can recede gracefully from it in conference. He may adopt a very weak or a very strong position on a certain issue to put himself in a better bargaining position at the conference. The larger the bag of tricks a chairman takes to conference, the more free play he has in the negotiation. For, though a conference is supposed to be a *resolution* of differences, the finished product is frequently a strange mélange of the original ingredients plus others not so easily defined.

We can draw some grim amusement from the loud hurly-burly which accompanies a bill through its initial stages, the countless hours of haggling in committee and on the Floor—for a comma or an adjective—and then observe the whole business disappear, swallowed up in a conference report.

There are good reasons for the phenomenon of bone-bruising Floor battles usually culminating in tranquil conference committee love affairs. The conference committee is the ultimate flowering of the power of seniority. For those who have followed these newsletters from the beginning I have sought to trace the interplay of forces at work here. There is cooperation. There is contention: the ins vs. the outs, the old boys vs. the new boys. Through it all we have been trying to perceive the locus of power.

The conference committee is the central core of the power. The Speaker's authority to appoint conferees is one of his most important prerogatives. He selects as members of the conference committee the senior members of the standing committee originating the legislation. He appoints the Democrats and Republicans. The conference committee meets in secret. No one who is not privy to the conference committee knows its workings. Away from prying eyes, any display of partisanship can be easily shed, as the comrades in arms from both sides recognize a mutuality of interest, and at the same time they may reaffirm the importance of seniority, the control of senior members. This is not to say there are no crushing conference committee battles. There are. But it takes a really big issue to disrupt the conference with an open battle.

This suggests another major function of the legislative process—synthesis, or perhaps a better word, distillation. Issues are synthesized, distilled. At each stage the pressures to conform are greater.

At each stage the partisan issue must be a large one to survive. At the conference stage most of the partisanship has been wrung out, and what remains is the seniors vs. the rest, the seniors in both parties who preside uneasily over the roiling mass below.

There are exceptions and, like most exceptions, they prove the rule. The School Bill passed the House last year, and the Rules Committee, in a fit of rebellion, refused to report out a Rule on appointment of conferees. The Speaker appoints conferees, but he does it with a Rule from the Rules Committee. The committee would not grant one on this important bill. While there were other reasons, it was also defiance and a demonstration of power. What should be noted, however, is the fact that the committee does not press this advantage too often. Wisely, the members, seniors all, realize that its exercise threatens seniority. Power exercised too often outside the regular order is power dissipated.

Very sincerely,

Clem Miller

CHAPTER IV

THE PARTY IN THE HOUSE

ONE OF the interesting things to watch in returns on congressional races is the emphasis placed on the relative strength that the Republican and Democratic parties will have in the new Congress. We were told before the 1960 election that it was impossible for the Republicans to gain control of the Senate but that there was a distinct possibility that they would regain control of the House. This did not happen. The Democrats emerged with what was called a good working majority. They elected the Speaker and organized the House; consequently Democrats had a majority in each committee, with the senior Democrat as chairman. They organized the Senate and won the White House. With these policy branches firmly in the hands of one party, it would seem logical to expect the Democrats to be able to implement any program they desired, but this has not been true. Party regularity is not the keystone of congressional operations. Liberals and conservatives are found in both parties. There are more conservatives in the Democratic party than there are liberals in the Republican party. Hence the "majority" of Democrats is more apparent than real. This has many potential pitfalls for the majority—most of which are lost to the lay observer.

"A political party is an organized group which attempts to gain control of a government through the process of elections." Such a definition is fairly standard. It excludes those groups which gain control through *coup d'état,* revolution, or craft. The party is a peaceful method of seizing power,[1] with the emphasis on the gaining of power or control as a result of deliberate organization. If the party is organized around a basic body of beliefs or philosophy, it is

[1] See E. E. Schattschneider, *Party Government,* (New York, 1942), Chapter III.

referred to as an ideological party. A party which can keep its members voting with some degree of regularity in line with this ideology, through a judicious use of rewards and punishments, is known as a party with internal responsibility.

If one examines the American national parties he will see that they are fairly well united in their efforts to elect the President and the Vice-President. But even with this quasi-unity there is no single ideology which pervades the parties—view the teams of Roosevelt and Garner, Eisenhower and Nixon, Kennedy and Johnson. The parties are not truly ideological; neither are they responsible.

With reference to the Presidency, the parties are national and do fit into the definition of a party in that they have an organization with the aim of gaining control of the government. The congressional parties subtract one essential element—they are not really organized with the specific aim of taking control of a government. Few campaigns are directed at the general idea of "My party, on a national basis stands for this, and this, and this. Do not consider me or my opponent as men, consider us only as members of a party. Vote for the party, not for the man!" On the contrary, congressmen are elected from 435 districts scattered across the fifty states. They share one thing in common—each represents a unique district. The needs, desires, and demands of each district are different. Therefore if a congressman truly represents his district, his responses to proposed legislation will not seem to follow a consistent pattern. He must choose between representing his district as he believes most people would want him to vote on an issue or (in case he thinks most of his district is wrong on an issue) voting his own ideas or those which fit into the broad ideological pattern of the majority of the members of his party in the House.

National party labels are desirable to a congressional candidate. It is often easier to be elected if one is associated at least in name with a party with a national name and heritage. Our party system makes it easier to organize Congress by setting up a framework, a regular pattern.

There is little effective party responsibility, and only those with strong personal beliefs—and perhaps relatively safe districts—can be said to be united ideologically. Many are simply inclined to vote their district.

These letters show something of the complexity of our party system as it operates in the House of Representatives.

Dear Friend:

Personalities and personal feeling play important roles in Washington politics. It is not the whole of the matter, however, as a recent popular novel would have us believe. In drawing the Washington scene entirely in terms of the interaction of personalities, the book misses by a country mile. Personal feeling played against the backboard of partisan party attitudes is what makes up what we call "politics."

Party attitudes are deep-set. They are traditional and historical. Personal feelings are transitory and fleeting, but they are also recurring. This can be decisive at the particular, crucial moment of legislative action. The reaction of John Q. Citizen to feeling in politics is ambivalent. He realizes that anger, affection, remorse, are the ingredients of daily life, he recognizes it in public life, he has it drummed into him by the daily press, but somehow he does not willingly accept it as a factor in arriving at public decisions. Headlines are always heralding histrionics and hysterics. Politicians are always "lashing out," "attacking bitterly," "reacting violently."

The fact is that political relationships are most generally conducted with far more restraint than these flamboyant accounts would indicate. When one takes the trouble to examine the mild words actually exchanged and observe the courtly manners exhibited, it is difficult to connect them with the headlines.

In order to account for these contradictions it is necessary to draw some distinctions. Debate on the Floor of the House is regarded differently by the Members than an extemporaneous speech before a partisan crowd at a clambake down home. We freely grant license in the latter not extended in the former.

There is plenty of general political warfare in the House, but the bounds between general attack and personalities are scrupulously observed by most. There is an escape valve available for those who must get personal without offending the House mores—the Appendix of the *Record*. This weird and wonderful coda on the daily record of Congress' proceedings is open to all, as many times as one desires. Anything, relevant or irrelevant, can be put in the Appendix.

Your most atavistic urges can be camouflaged behind some bitter editorial, all duly printed without objection.

There are those who indulge in personalities despite the rules, and they are well known. Even their more general statements become clothed in personal feeling reaching a stage of vindictiveness, which acquires for them an undesirable reputation.

We might define another form of emotional bloodletting too. This is the tendency to get in on every debate, have a word to say on every subject. It can be a fatal disease. One rarely speaks up on subjects outside his "specialty." It makes the congressman appear bizarre or ridiculous.

So, there is restraint in Congress to a rather remarkable degree, in spite of what may seem to be the contrary. There are several reasons why this is so. First, there is the compelling need for respect—to be held in respectful esteem by your colleagues. It can and does constitute a most restraining force. Aside from your seniority on committee—and to begin with, you have no seniority —this respect by colleagues is almost your only leverage. When a bill of great importance to a Member is in process, he wants to be able to hear, "I'll vote for it because it's Jim's bill. Jim's a great guy," not "If Jim's for it, I'm against it, that————." If good feeling has been thrown away with distasteful contention and indiscriminate commentary, the esteem won't be there when it's needed. This sensitivity makes Congress something less of a bedlam than is supposed. It inhibits one from saying a lot of things, many of which actually need saying.

The facts are that one does not get personal. One confines his vitriol for the hustings down home and for the Appendix. One also sticks to his knitting—tending to his own committee work and defending his home district before other committees. This may have the effect of making Congress more conservative than it really is. As one gains seniority, these rules of conduct to achieve personal esteem grow progressively less important. The power factor of time in service overwhelms the adverse effect of making a fool of oneself, until a senior congressman is almost immune from criticism no matter what he does.

Now, as to personal overindulgence, it is worth noting that the impulse usually founders on political necessity. One may wish to show personal pique by saying something cutting on the Floor (suitably camouflaged to avoid open breach with the rules) or by an adverse vote, but the Member hesitates to follow through because it runs counter to his more basic political philosophy. One may want to get even for some slight, but he is reasonably certain he will have to eat his words when the time for the roll call arrives. His sense of party responsibility or allegiance to his constituents then stays his hand. It is a rare event when someone permits his personal feelings to interfere with his commitment on a major bill.

We have our share of dogs-in-the-manger, backbiters, dyspeptics, gossips and low-boilers, just as in any other walk of life. And everyone recognizes that in the heat of debate, the stage is set for a display of high feeling. When events veer toward the personal, the results can be unfortunate. A Member of Congress who in his zeal puts words in a committee chairman's mouth, accuses another Member in a personal way, or impugns the other party, is only hurting himself. He not only risks losing a few votes, but he suffers an invalidism in the eyes of his peers from which it will be difficult or impossible to recover. He may not even be aware of it, masked behind the cordiality which is our way of life.

As a Member seeks out the means of "getting even" for some real or imaginary slight, he lives with the certainty that the day will come when it can be returned with interest. So, he generally discards the impulse to be recriminating, even if a good opportunity arises, and he lives with his exasperations, dreaming of the foolproof revenge that never comes.

This decision is not particularly special nor at all unique because everyone exercises self-imposed restraint on his conduct. It is worth reporting simply because it does not readily come through in news accounts. In the course of the legislative process there is a great deal of surface froth, confusing because it appears to be the real thing. It is hard to separate conduct permissible outside the halls from that which is inexcusable within; to separate the permissive generalized assault from the personalized; to separate keen debate in your "field" from the undisciplined roving into many others; and finally to discern how emotions must fit into the partisan atmosphere of our Capitol. These distinctions are important for an understanding of how Congress works. It is also important for a Member to know the rules, because he tampers with them at his peril.

Very sincerely,

Clem Miller

Dear Friend:

As this session nears a close every news correspondent is sharpening his pencil for a spate of articles on the effectiveness of the Congress. The unflagging conclusion, thus far, is that the Democrats have not delivered on the promise of their last November majority. Robert Spivack of the *New York Post* says in *The Nation*: ". . . the rapidity of public disenchantment with Congressional Democrats since the party's impressive showing at the polls barely a year ago ranks as something of a political phenomenon."

To me, for the House of Representatives, at any rate, this does not seem to be as much of a phenomenon as it apparently is to the Spivacks. What the correspondents need to do is to sit down with a stubby pencil and do some simple addition and subtraction. What we will find is that the combination of southern Democrats and northern Republicans can always squeak out a majority when they want to, and they want to on a great number of significant issues.

There are 283 Democrats in Congress. There are 160 northern Democrats and roughly 99 southern Democrats. (This includes Texas but does not include the border states of Maryland, West Virginia, Kentucky, and Missouri, which generally cancel each other out. Maryland votes against us, West Virginia with us, Missouri cancels itself out, half liberal, half southern, and Kentucky, ambivalent, sometimes with us and sometimes against us.) There were 63 new Democratic congressmen elected last November. Thirteen replaced Democrats who were retiring for one reason or another and 50 replaced Republicans. Actually, the Democratic party as nonsoutherners define it is a minority in the House. Begin with a base of 160

	85TH CONGRESS (1957-1958)	86TH CONGRESS (1959-1960)
Total Democrats (election date)	234	283
Northern Democrats with 50 percent border state	116	175
Southern Democrats with 50 percent border state	118	108
Republicans	201	154

northern Democratic votes. Add to it fifty percent of the border state Democrats. We are always 15 to 30 votes shy, depending on the 10 southern votes and 10 to 20 Republican votes for the difference.

If we can't even produce a majority, the prospect of overriding a veto becomes an absurdity. I fail to find any evidence that the newsmen have been able to give expression to these simple facts. While everyone is aware of the southern Democrat-Republican line-up, and it gets frequent reference, there seems to be no ability to relate it to the November sweep of last year. The sweep is always treated as a phenomenon *in vacuo*.

Let us now recap, using the vote on the Landrum-Griffin Labor Bill as an example:

Total vote *for* Landrum-Griffin	229
Total vote *against* Landrum-Griffin	201
Northern Democrats *against* Landrum-Griffin	154
Northern Democrats *for* Landrum-Griffin	4
Southern Democrats *for* Landrum-Griffin	84
Southern Democrats *against* Landrum-Griffin	13
Border State Democrats *against* Landrum-Griffin	17
Border State Democrats *for* Landrum-Griffin	13
Total Republicans *against* Landrum-Griffin	17

Play with these figures as you will, the fact emerges that the liberal Democrats simply don't have the votes.

Next, I might mention the inevitable sectional differences. Where there is a working majority, sectional disagreements can be smothered in the overall vote. However, without a true working majority these sectional variations become determinants. The result is an unpredictable vote. For example, the wheat bill should have gone through. With our uneasy majority, the decisive votes were cast against the bill by a few big-city congressmen who have supported the Democratic farm program in the past but who are increasingly restive and unhappy. So the bill lost.

There are fascinating interrhythms to these roll call examinations. It is profitable to study just the agricultural votes as an example of regional differences. For example, note the number of tobacco congressmen whose bill just squeaked through, who then turned around and voted against the wheat bill. Or there was the solid West Virginia vote against TVA—spite perhaps, but dictated by the plight of that state, beset by the unemployment in the coal fields.

Finally affecting any vote is the defection of individuals for one reason or another. It has been said that the most powerful lobby in Congress is one congressman lobbying another. A convinced Member can perhaps take several other Members with him on a particular vote. I intend to deal further with this in another letter.

Of course, as the issue looms larger and more is at stake, the private interests and influences fall away before the massive forces at work.

Very sincerely,

Clem Miller

Dear Friend:

The debate over civil rights in the House has now concluded. It consumed ten working days in the House; the speeches take up 627 pages in the *Congressional Record* but it is doubtful if a single vote was changed through the entire course. Other work in the House came almost to a complete standstill while the matter pended. This leads many to the erroneous conclusion that the debate was a waste of time. But it was not.

The debate on civil rights furnished the essential flux which forged all the vague, generalized talk into hard, congressional policy. As we have noted, the pressure behind most major legislation builds and builds for years. Usually, in spite of this head of steam, it is not till you get right into the debate itself that the fundamental lines are drawn, or that the various proposals are given close, concentrated attention.

The sequence of events here is instructive. The Civil Rights Commission, appointed in 1957, furnished the starting point with the rather unexpected recommendations of September, 1959. Congressman ——— incorporated the Commission's recommendation on elections into a bill designated as the voting registrant proposal. It excited immediate academic attention in the law schools. Doubts as to the constitutionality and efficacy of the provisions were transmitted to the Attorney General who came forward with the voting referee proposal; it was placed before the House by the ranking Republican of the Judiciary Committee.

Immediately, this Republican proposal came under scrutiny. During Senate debate, two Democratic senators produced new ideas in a bill (the "enrollment officer" plan) which would overcome the constitutional and administrative doubts about the Republican proposals.

Up to the time of the debate, the South contented itself with simple unrelieved hostility. Once debate was joined, however, its excellent lawyers began a painstaking analysis of the two proposals. Through the debate, their keen observations and close criticisms resulted in modification here and tailoring there, until the final form was reached.

Let us look briefly at the situation as it existed before debate began. Southerners and Republicans had concluded that the subject would never come to the Floor during this session. The Democratic bill was believed pigeonholed in the Rules Committee.

To get around the Rules Committee, the Judiciary Committee Chairman filed a discharge petition but it was expected to languish short of the 219 signatures necessary for consideration. During January the signatures began to mount. Finally, when the 190 mark was reached—with less than 30 more needed to bring the measure to the Floor—the Republican Attorney General acted, excoriating the enrollment officer proposal, and presented us with the referee system. The Rules Committee suddenly granted a Rule. If the measure came to the Floor with benefit of a Rule, the Rules Committee could control its terms; but if it came by means of the discharge petition, terms of the debate would be dictated by the Judiciary Committee. The Rule granted was unique in living memory. In effect, it permitted only the referee amendment. Thus, the pattern was set for the most bizarre alignment of forces seen in the House during this (and perhaps many another) session of Congress. Republicans, who had quietly helped to sit on civil rights, now had to parade their colors as official champions. Since this was their unwilling role, they were going to demand a full measure of credit.

Exposed for the world to see was the three-party Congress. Even debate time was tripartite. The fifteen hours were divided—five to Republicans, five to northern Democrats, and five to southern Democrats. The Republicans had their usual table to the left of the Speaker, the southerners occupied the center table, and the northern Democrats the right.

From the very start it was readily apparent that if there were to be a civil rights bill, it would have to be Republican and written in Republican terms. If the Republican amendment were not accepted they would have no other, and civil rights might go down the drain.

Led by a certain congressman, northern Democrats wanted a bill, *any* bill that might work, and were hence prepared to deliver many hostages to get one. When a Member from the South, in a masterful presentation on the second day, began punching holes in the Republican amendment, some northern Democrats began having serious doubts as to its practicality and legality. I think the Judiciary Chairman himself began to have doubts. These very doubts pushed the Democratic proposal for enrollment officers into the forefront. Overtures were made to increase its palatability by giving it to the Republicans free of charge, the name of the Democratic originator to be supplanted by one of their own choosing. But it was "no sale" for the Minority Leader. It must be the Republican amendment or *nothing*.

In the most dramatic moment of the debate these outlines were etched in bold relief. Rebuffed by the Republicans, the Democrats offered a substitute amendment. The Floor was placid with the certainty of failure as a case was made for the amendment. Immediately, in a bold foray, the southerners were thrown in with us to support the amendment. A second vote had to be taken, and the southerners were held with us, but you could see the chagrin working in their faces. They clustered excitedly around their leader, an unmoving, stooped old man, as he stood by the mike at his desk, his eyes darting around the room, just the faintest trace of a smile on his lips.

A third test of our amendment had to be suffered through. The southern leaders were pleading with their fellows, hanging on their arms. The southerners were seething. They seemed to be unable to grasp the strategy; they could not believe it to be so. They wavered irresolutely. The Republicans were about to troop up the aisle through the tellers united. Finally, the southerners broke toward the teller aisle. One of their leaders planked himself across one of the aisles, seeming to hold back his friends with a physical barricade.

If there was dismay among the southerners, there was consternation among the Republicans. Their strategy of "ours or nothing" had worked with the Judiciary Chairman, but it would not work with the southern chief. He was as implacable as was the Minority Leader. Divining the Republicans' intentions, the southern leader had set out to get *no* bill by joining with us on our amendment. Then they had planned to team with the Republicans on passage against *any* bill. The irresoluteness of the southerners saved the day for the Minority Leader. While pandemonium raged in the shambles which had been made, the scene on the Floor was a seething confusion. The author of the Republican amendment broke from an angry knot in the well of the House, waving a piece of paper which he handed to the reading clerk. It was, he said, a "different" amendment. The Chairman of the CWH ruled that it was "different" and in order. The bill proceeded on its certain way with the "new" amendment.

Very sincerely,

Clem Miller

Dear Friend:

The debate over civil rights did have an aftermath, but how permanent the effect will be is difficult to ascertain at this time. We should note some transient effects, however.

The debate made the tripartite nature of the House stand out in bold relief. Southerners announced that the South might select independent electors for President. Southern congressmen were urged to refuse to join the northerners in organizing the House in 1961. Since they had been trampled on they would retaliate wherever it would be effective. For the first time, they had felt the chilling breeze of a hostile coalition, and it was not to their liking. It remains to be seen whether the alliance between southerners and Republicans can be re-formed. Standing behind the rail during the debate, listening to the southerners' comments, we could see that reluctance to cast their lot formally with the Republicans runs very deep. It may be difficult for their leaders to hold the reins. Ninety-three voted against the Rule for the Civil Rights Bill.

Meantime, delay and intransigence are the principal weapons. The Rules Committee permits time to run on while major bills back up. With the self-assured extended deliberateness obtained during many years in the legislative wars, its Chairman delays, postpones, and puts off—as if to tell us that Civil Rights or no, his view is going to prevail.

Against this massive obstacle, the northern Democrats steer their uncertain course. The Democratic Study Group, composed of northern liberal Democrats outgunned by the results of the Landrum-Griffin Bill just as the southerners were on civil rights, forms a spearhead for liberal legislation. Or would closer description say that it constitutes a counterweight for the use of the Leadership? Propulsive or kinetic? It is difficult to say.

On significant matters that are far enough along in the legislative process, the Speaker now consults with the DSG Chairman. Is it the threat of liberal power or liberal veto which lies behind this attention? Or is our chairman sought out in order to counterbalance the effect of the southern-Republican alliance? The Leadership, using now one bill, then another, appeals to forces within the factions that will unsettle and unsteady them, and hence make them more malleable. Probably the Leadership would feel better without the DSG, but now that it is a fact, it must be used and dealt with, perhaps advantageously like all other political realities.

The DSG took shape last September, with meetings to establish a firm purpose and to decide on objectives and structure. There was effort to avoid formal opposition to the Leadership. Emphasis was placed on allegiance to the Democratic party platform. The group believed that the Leadership would welcome such organization, but that it could not present us with a formal blessing. Thus it began, not under a cloud, but not smiled on either—neither in, nor way out.

A whip system was set up whereby members could be quickly brought to the Floor through a chain of phone calls. Agreement was reached on eight specific legislative objectives, bills already in the main stream but held up by the Rules Committee. After much consideration of the intricacies of regional differences, the group agreed on an executive committee of nine and a steering committee of twenty-one.

The name "Democratic Study Group" was adopted so its activities could not be tagged as oppositional. An office was set up and two staff members were designated to plan, to research the issues, and to coordinate the diverse interests. All this was in the closing days of September. The group was ready for business in January, 1960. As the year has worn on, some success has been achieved. During the civil rights debate, DSG meetings furnished the fulcrum for northern policy. During the flurry over raising the interest rate, the Leadership was startled when a large group was assembled on two hours notice; this resulted in a second look at the bill and eventual withdrawal of Leadership support. On legislation such as the Area Redevelopment Bill, the School Aid Bill, and the Forand Bill, the Chairman of the DSG is now among those to whom the Leadership looks in the constant negotiation for position and fulfillment.

Very sincerely,

Clem Miller

CHAPTER V
SPECIAL INTEREST GROUPS

GROUPS which are organized to influence the activities of government at all levels are called interest groups, pressure groups, or lobbies—or perhaps unprintable names—depending upon one's personal prejudices. Usually there is an inward if not an outward feeling of dislike and distrust of these groups regardless of what they are called.

These special interest groups differ from political parties in that they are not seeking to control government through the process of elections but are attempting rather to influence the activities of those who are elected or who serve in administrative positions in the executive and legislative branches. To be sure, interest groups support, endorse, and contribute to the campaign funds of candidates, but they do not nominate candidates and they do not organize Congress after elections. Despite what newspapers, radio, and television might lead one to think, there are no NAM-Chamber of Commerce candidates for congressional seats. Neither are there AFofL-CIO candidates. Political parties supply the candidates and organize the Congress.

Americans have a stereotyped picture of the representatives of the various special interests which make up the whole of our country; they are unsavory characters who lie, bribe, threaten, and entertain to achieve their ends. These ends are always "special," and for that reason we tend to assume that they are contrary to the general public interest.

Stereotypes seldom fit any one or even a group of individuals. There are those representatives of special interests who may, in part, match this stereotype. Most interest representatives do not. They range from those groups which are highly organized on a national basis such as the American Legion, the National Association of Manufacturers, the United States Chamber of Commerce, the AFofL-CIO, the Farm Bureau Federation, and the National Council of Churches down to small groups of poultry producers or pecan growers. Each has its own problems and each feels that government action, inaction, or retreat from action in its own sphere of interest is in the general public interest.

Such pressure groups, and others like them, are essential to the American political process. They seem to thrive particularly in a system which lacks responsible ideological parties. They serve many useful purposes. They make certain that a congressman has all of the relevant facts about every aspect of every issue in which they are interested. They keep him in touch with the interests in his district. They keep the people at home informed of the actions of their congressman. In short, they are generally neither sinister nor malicious, and they do deserve to be understood.

Dear Friend:

I have just returned to Washington after two months in the district, meeting with friends, strangers, and even a foe or two. It was an exhilarating experience. The reception was cordial and the interest genuine. I attended about 176 meetings of one sort or another, and spoke (and listened) an average of three times a day, seven days a week, for more than eight weeks. At the end I felt rather talked out. (Politicians, however, rebound quickly; I will be talking to a poultry association in New York next week.)

I often talked quite generally on the nature of Congress, much in the vein I have taken in these letters. I found audiences of all kinds interested in the workings of Congress. I found others who felt that I present too pessimistic a view. The usual expressed reaction was one of welcoming my effort to be candid. We have been taking our pap sugar-coated for so long. From reading reports of what my confreres were doing in their own bailiwicks, this "laying it on the line" in frank congressman-constituent discussions may become a national pastime.

I am not sure that I saw much evidence of a growing concern for our national, public needs, or a willingness to grapple with today's hard-nut problems at home. It is depressing to observe how fear of "controversy" has sapped our ability to take a look at and talk about our most important problems.

Perhaps it is not remarkable, but school children asked the most searching questions. They asked unaffectedly about the future, war or peace, the atom. Adults rarely referred to these greater issues in discussion, though the concern of their children was perhaps an index of their fundamental concerns. Occasionally, I was asked by adults about such relatively superficial topics as Khrushchev's visit, and why Congress ducked him. This rather pointed avoidance of issues which may in reality most profoundly affect their future, and that of their children, really amazed me.

The outlines of my trip were determined by those groups which sought meetings. There was good focus on our district bread-and-butter needs—flood control, harbor development, wine grape inspection, and so on—and many meetings with service clubs.

Our economy in the district is showing mixed signs. There are signals of impending troubles in the lumber industry, and in agriculture generally. Shortage of mortgage money in housing is already having its first effects on lumber and related businesses, and the attendant anxieties transmit readily to congressmen. In the portion of my district where the office and government workers (the last and least affected by economic slowdowns) are dominant, I heard little complaint.

In addition to talking and listening to district economic-interest groups, I was also engaged continuously in the job of being a representative of individuals. I collected lists of problems on which individuals asked valid intercession with their impersonal, bureaucratic government—pensions, social security, civil service, and so on. Personal problems large and small, they are all important to the possessor. Here was an added dimension to my earlier tours as a candidate.

This extra responsibility leads to problems because friends of campaigning days are hurt. It is impossible to explain that strangers' demands on your time are so great that time is not left for one's own personal calls. However, I made it a point to talk personally with any individual who sought a meeting for whatever reason.

A great deal of my time was spent in talking about how the grass-roots can be more effective in Washington. We keep forgetting that this is a representative government. This is not only true of the legislators themselves, but as life becomes more fragmented, there must be representation of the fragments. Good (representative, responsive, responsible) lobbies become more essential. I tried to tell people the differences between good lobbies and bad, and what to do about them.

I told the physicians and the lumbermen that as far as I could see, much of their lobbying—at the national level, at least—was poor. I told the teachers their lobbying was generally effective.

Many people were extremely interested in learning how they

could be more effective citizens. This was most encouraging to me. I got the idea that if people only knew how they could be more effective, they would do something about it. It appears that people are not so much cynical about their government as they are full of feelings of insignificance and impotence.

Very sincerely,

Clem Miller

Dear Friend:

In today's world most people are ready to admit that, as much as they dislike the word "lobbying," the function carried on under this name is essential to government. (In fact, the right to lobby is protected by the First Amendment.) In recent months there has been a graphic contrast here in effectiveness of lobbying activity between two segments of agriculture important to the economic health of our district: walnut growers and poultrymen. Both groups are in economic trouble because of abundance.

The walnut growers have a large carry-over from last year which, if placed on top of this year's record production, would break the market. The growers wanted the government to buy walnuts for diversion into the school lunch program, to be financed from existing tariffs on foreign walnut imports.

In the poultry industry, overproduction led by huge combines of bankers and feed companies, with million-hen farms, has broken the egg and meat-bird markets wide open. Independent poultrymen are losing six to eight cents per dozen eggs and four to eight cents per pound of meat, and are going bankrupt in droves.

The walnut industry is well organized. They have been proud that they don't have supports and don't ask the government for "handouts." This is easy to understand. One marketing cooperative controls seventy per cent of the state's production. So, when the industry got in trouble and came to Washington, they came well prepared. Each California congressman received a personal, carefully reasoned, five-page letter. It was followed up by another, shorter letter. Then, a telegram called attention to the letters. Finally, there was a telephone call, asking for comments on the letters. By this time, we were fairly wide awake. Quite properly, the group worked through the congressman in whose district the association offices and many growers are located. We received several calls from the congressman's staff, alerting us, keeping us posted, offering help in answering questions.

After this preliminary barrage, the walnut growers' representative was ready to come to town. He set up headquarters at a nearby hotel. He called on congressmen several times, accompanied by a gentleman from the packing and canning section of the industry. He talked to my legislative assistant. Then we were all invited to a luncheon at the hotel, where the plight of the industry was laid before us and it was announced that a meeting was set up with the Secretary of Agriculture. Meticulous care was taken to be sure that all congressmen and senators who represent walnut growers would be there. In a large Department of Agriculture conference room with numerous department officials present, a skillful "presentation" for the industry was made. Immediately afterward, the walnut congressmen jumped up to demand action. One was self-contained but bitter about department inaction. Another pointed out the illogical Administration position in caustic terms. In turn, each congressman added his bit to the complaint. The Administration was bland and quite self-righteous ("We have more confidence in the walnut grower than he has in himself."). The exasperation of the Republican congressmen toward the Republican Secretary of Agriculture mounted. "Would a 'shaded' market price have to become a rout before the government moved?" they wanted to know. Administration officials were apparently unshaken.

However, two weeks later, the Administration did act. The industry was delighted. The work of the lobby had been effective.

Let's contrast this with the way things are developing in the egg industry. Some time ago I received a long letter from a constituent asking what congressional action was expected in poultry. A check revealed that nothing was contemplated in Congress. Of the seven thousand bills in Congress, there was not one on poultry or eggs. No hearings were scheduled. My interest piqued, I discussed the situation with House Agriculture Committee staff members and with the acting chairman of the subcommittee. The prevailing view was that since there was no leadership in the industry, and no agreement on policy, hearings would serve no purpose. I urged that hearings be scheduled to see if policy might materialize. A day or so later, I heard that a group of distressed poultrymen from New

Jersey were asking to meet with their government. The Georgia and Alabama broiler people also asked to be heard.

All of a sudden, we learned that there was to be a hearing. Citizens were petitioning their government for a redress of grievances. At the hearing a crowd of two hundred poultrymen swarmed into the Agriculture Committee room which had been designed for about seventy-five people. Poultrymen-witnesses testified that the lowest prices in eighteen years for eggs and chickens were bankrupting an industry. As one witness said, in 1957 we were separating the men from the boys; in 1959 it was the men from the giants. One poultryman gave a stark, moving account of his town's plight. He gestured to his friends, sitting somberly at his side. They had been against federal help until a month or so previously, he said. "We called the people who were down here in 1957 looking for handouts 'radicals.' Now, we are here ourselves."

Throughout two days the same depressing story was recounted as the farmer-witnesses, speaking for themselves and other small producers, took their turn. Technological advances, together with banker-feed company-grower integration, were destroying the independent poultryman. Then the Department of Agriculture spokesman told its story. He confirmed the growers' story but indicated that nothing could be done. It was the inexorable law of supply and demand. Significantly absent were representatives of the larger organized farm groups. At nightfall, the poultrymen had to return to their farms.

What was the next step? It is up to the interested congressmen, they told us. How come, we asked? What are we to do? The leader of the poultrymen said that we had been told the problem. Yes, was the response, but he and his friends should go to see the Secretary of Agriculture. Testimony had indicated that Congress had already given the Secretary all of the authority he needed to act. It would do no good to pass more laws, particularly since they would certainly end with Presidential vetoes.

All of the men were active poultrymen who had to get back to their flocks. They were leaving that night. Who was to carry the ball for them here in Washington during the next critical weeks? Who was going to do the telephoning? Who was going to coordinate policy between New Jersey, California, Alabama, Wisconsin, Georgia, and Kansas? The answer from them was, "No one." We had been given a problem. It was ours now. The result to date: a resolution of the Agriculture Committee urging the Secretary to "implement such programs of purchase, diversion, and export of poultry products as will lead toward improvement of the present critical situation." Results for the poultrymen: nothing.

Very sincerely,

Clem Miller

CONGRESS:
ITS ORGANIZATION AND
ROUTINE

OF THE many functions performed by the Congress of the United States, lawmaking is basic. Although the general voter is interested in how well the congressman represents his district in dealings with executive agencies and is excited by congressional investigations into various facets of American life (especially when hearings are televised), he considers his congressman primarily a lawmaker. Even so, there is widespread ignorance about the structure of Congress and the vital influence of human elements on the process of developing an idea into a law.

THE ORGANIZATION OF CONGRESS

Article I, Section 1 of the Constitution provides that "All legislative powers herein granted shall be vested in a Congress of the United States, which shall consist of a Senate and a House of Representatives."

The Senate is composed of one hundred members, two from each state. Originally, Senators represented their state governments; they were elected by the state legislatures. However, since the passage of the Seventeenth Amendment in 1913, Senators have been elected directly by the people.

The Constitution specifies that a Senator must be thirty years of age, must have been a citizen of the United States for nine years, and when elected, must be a resident of the state from which he is elected. Senators serve for staggered terms of six years, with one-third of the entire body elected every two years. In case of a vacancy in the Senate, a successor either is appointed by the governor of the state entitled to the seat or is elected by the people of that state in a special election. The new Senator serves until the next general election, when a successor is chosen to fill the unexpired term of the Senator whose seat has been vacated.

The House of Representatives is composed of 435 members elected every two years, the number from each state allocated on the basis of its population minus untaxed Indians. (Following the census of 1910, the total number of Representatives was set at 435. It has remained stable with the exception of a temporary increase in 1958 to 437 when Alaska and Hawaii were admitted to the union. The number returned to 435 in the redistribution which followed the 1960 census.) The Constitution guarantees every state at least one Representative and also says that there shall not be more than one Representative for each 30,000 of the population. Because of the increase in population, the latter restriction has become strictly historical since the size of the House remains unchanged. The Representatives come from districts which range in population from 159,099 to 806,701. In addition, one Ohio congressman, elected at large, represents 9,706,394 people. Despite the size of some of these districts, increasing the membership of the House would not solve anything because it is now unwieldy—and at times relies on *sub rosa* organization to accomplish its job.

A Representative must be at least twenty-five years old, must have been a citizen for seven years, and must be a resident of the state when elected but not necessarily of the district from which he is elected. If a vacancy occurs in the House, the Constitution states that the governor of the state from which the Representative came shall call a special election to elect a successor to serve out the remaining term of office, but in this case "shall" has been interpreted "may" and an election is often not held.

In addition to the 435 regular members of the House, there is also a Resident Commissioner from Puerto Rico authorized by the Congress in 1917. He enjoys most of the prerogatives of the Representatives, with the important exception that he cannot vote on legislation.

Any form of legislative action must be introduced into one house or the other by a member of the Congress, though he need not initiate the idea, write up the document, or even agree with its contents.

Approximately eighty percent of the public bills passed by any session of Congress have their genesis in the executive branch of the government. The President is required by the Constitution to deliver a message to the Congress on the state of the union, and he is authorized to appear before the Congress or to send messages to them from time to time suggesting courses of action. Some Presidents have not been as "strong" as others. That is to say, some have conceived of the Presidency as essentially an administrative position and their role as policy maker to be practically nonexistent. The "strong" Presidents have been aggressive and have shouldered the major responsibility for initiating policy and for attempting to get Congress to act on that policy. This kind of leadership is apparently expected of a President today; even congressmen criticize the President if he does not tell them completely what he wants, if he does not exercise "Presidential leadership." A formal communication to Congress is often accompanied by a draft of the legislation proposed by the President. This draft is referred to the proper committee and the chairman or one of the members will present the bill formally. The administrative departments and agencies also have friends in Congress who will gladly introduce legislation. Such bills are often the result of lengthy study by the administrator and his staff and may be highly technical, but still must be brought before Congress by a member of the House or of the Senate.

Members of Congress also submit legislation which is the result of their own ideas, perhaps springing from basic convictions or from campaign promises. Or a Representative may discover after he is in office some area of public or private activity which needs regulation or needs freedom from regulation. He is free to think strictly in terms of his ideas and of the needs of his constituents as he sees them.

Constituents often provide the congressman with legislative ideas. An individual may petition him to introduce a private bill to pay for damages which he has suffered at the hands of the government or its employees. One of the pressure groups in his district or state may ask him to introduce a piece of legislation which it has drawn up. Action proposed by such a group may be in complete agreement with the views of the congressman, and in such a case he is happy to file the proposal with the Congress. If he does not agree with the action proposed he will probably bring the matter before Congress anyway, with the statement that he is introducing the measure "by request."

Thousands of proposals for action are submitted to each session of Congress. Many will never be acted upon. Those fortunate enough to warrant consideration will be in one of the following four forms:

1. *The Bill.*[1] The bill is by far the most customary form used by members of both houses for legislation, whether permanent or temporary, general or special, public or private. Bills may originate in either house, with the exception specified in the Constitution that all bills which raise revenue shall begin in the House of Representatives.

As it is introduced, each bill is designated "H. R." (House of Representatives) or "S." (Senate), to indicate where it originated, and is numbered. All bills follow a similar pathway, to be described more in detail later. Some will become law; others will die along the way. A bill becomes a law after it is agreed upon by both houses and is signed by the President or allowed to become effective without his signature; if the President vetoes a measure, it will become law anyway if the veto is overridden by a two-thirds majority in both houses.

2. *The Joint Resolution.*[2] A joint resolution accomplishes the same ends as a bill and goes through the same procedures except for the joint resolution which proposes an amendment to the Con-

[1] See page 168 for an example of a bill.
[2] See page 169 for an example of a joint resolution.

stitution, in which case the President is by-passed. When passed by both houses, the proposed amendment is forwarded directly to the Administrator of General Services, who must submit it to the states for their action.

A joint resolution is designated "H. J. Res." or "S. J. Res." and numbered.

3. *The Concurrent Resolution.*[3] Unlike a bill or a joint resolution, the concurrent resolution does not become a law and is not submitted to the President for his action. It is used to handle matters affecting the operation of the two houses and may be used to express the position, opinions, or desires of the Congress. It is identified by "H. Con. Res." or "S. Con. Res." and its number. If it is adopted by both houses, it is signed by the Clerk of the House and the Secretary of the Senate and is published as a special part of the Statutes at Large.

4. *Simple Resolutions.*[4] Each house of Congress manages its own internal business. If a matter arises concerning the operation of either house alone, it is initiated by a simple resolution in that house. Each one is numbered, preceded by "H. Res." or "S. Res." A simple resolution is considered only by the house concerned and if passed is signed by the appropriate officer and is published in the *Congressional Record.*

COMMITTEES DO THE SPADEWORK

Most of the work of Congress, because of its size and the mass of detailed legislation, must be carried on through committees. There are several types of committees in Congress. In the legislative process, the most important of these are the standing or permanent committees. Since the Legislative Reorganization Act of 1946, the number of these committees has been reduced; at the present time there are nineteen in the House of Representatives and fifteen in the Senate. Each committee has jurisdiction over specific

[3] See page 165 for an example of a concurrent resolution.
[4] See page 167 for an example of a simple resolution.

areas of legislation, e.g., the Committee on Foreign Affairs in the House and the Committee on Foreign Relations in the Senate. These committees are further divided into subcommittees which consider more specialized aspects of a bill referred to the whole committee. These standing committees are the "work horses" of Congress and can largely determine the fate of a bill which they consider; sometimes the chairman almost alone can determine whether a bill shall live or die. Additionally, there are several standing joint committees which are made up of members from both houses. Of these, only the Joint Committee on Atomic Energy may report legislation to the Floor of Congress for consideration.

Temporary committees may be appointed to perform a single function and then cease to exist after the job has been completed. Of this type is the special or select committee, usually set up to investigate a particular area of activity with the assumed purpose of determining the need for legislation in that area. When the investigation has been completed or the appropriation has been spent, the committee ceases to exist. President Truman gained a national reputation when he was a Senator from Missouri and headed the Truman Committee which investigated war contracts. Senator Estes Kefauver achieved national fame through his often televised investigations of organized crime. Neither of these committees exists today.

The joint conference committee which meets to iron out the differences between the two houses after they have passed a bill in slightly different forms is another type of temporary committee. The best example of this activity takes place when an appropriation bill has passed both houses but with differing amounts appropriated. More will be said of this committee later.

The Committee of the Whole House on the State of the Union exists only in the House of Representatives, and is composed of all the members of that house. In order to expedite legislation at times, the Representatives assemble as a committee of the whole and then are adjourned on completion of the work specifically before them.

One other type of committee is often considered as permanent but does not enter directly into the legislative process by considering proposed legislation and reporting on it. This is the "permanent" investigating committee, of which the House Committee on Un-American Activities is an example. This type of committee technically belongs in the category of special or select committees, for each must be reconsidered with each session of Congress and a special appropriation must be made for its continuance. However, many have become more or less permanent congressional fixtures.

FROM PROPOSED BILL TO LAW

A detailed description of the path a bill must follow will give us an essential, though mechanical, view of the legislative process.

Introduction in the House. A bill must be introduced by a Member, Delegate, or Resident Commissioner. It may be introduced at any time the House is in session simply by dropping a bill into the "hopper" at the desk of the Clerk of the House. The title of the bill is then entered in the *Journal* and is printed in the *Congressional Record*. The Clerk of the House assigns the bill its legislative number.

Introduction in the Senate. A more formal procedure is followed in the Senate. At a time set aside for such matters a Senator rises, states that he has a bill to be offered, and sends it to the desk of the Secretary of the Senate by a page. In the Senate the bill is read by title only, then the title is entered in the *Journal* and is printed in the *Congressional Record*.

From this point, we will follow the path of a bill which originated in the House through the House procedure, then through the Senate, to conference committee, and to the President.

LEGISLATION AND THE HOUSE OF REPRESENTATIVES

1. *Reference to Committee.* The Speaker of the House, with the assistance of the Parliamentarian, assigns the bill to a standing

committee. Usually the assignment is simple; in some cases this may be complex and the assignment to a particular committee in preference to some other may well determine whether the bill will ever be reported out of committee to the Floor. For example, should a bill on taxing a foodstuff be sent to the committee which considers taxes, or should it be sent to the committee which considers legislation concerning food? The decision of the Speaker may be appealed if the issue is vital enough to the Representative to risk incurring the Speaker's wrath. Such appeal is infrequent and is seldom successful.

2. *Consideration by the Standing Committee.* The chairman of the committee to which the bill is sent sets the machinery in motion. He may, on his own or at the request of the sponsor of the bill, refer it to a subcommittee for more specialized consideration. A copy of the bill is sent immediately to the executive agency which will have the responsibility for administering the act if it becomes law, requesting a report on the need for or desirability of such a law. Time is allowed for such reports to come in and they are considered by the committee, but they are only advisory and in no legal way determine the course of action of the committee. These reports are requested of the executive agency even when different parties control the Congress and the executive branch of the government.

If the bill is important, rather than just routine, and particularly if it is controversial, the committee will usually set a date for public hearings. If the committee desires to hear the opinions of specific persons, they will be requested to appear or may if necessary be issued a subpoena. Interest groups and private citizens who have an interest in the bill may be scheduled to appear. A limited number of seats are allotted for the public to witness the hearings.

The hearing usually begins with a complete reading of the bill, followed by remarks by the committee chairman and, typically, by the ranking member of the opposition party. Those who are to testify are then called, with members of the House and the Senate given priority, followed by high officers of the executive branch and the military, and so on down the line until all have been heard or until the committee feels that it has enough information to make a decision on the bill. Some of the witnesses follow prepared statements and consume much time in expanding them. Others appear briefly and simply state their views and respond to questions. All the testimony is included in the record and is published.

If the hearing is on a confidential subject, or if the committee feels that a witness and his testimony must be protected, executive sessions, not open to the public or to newsmen, may be held. There are also times when hearings on a bill might have unfortunate political repercussions; such hearings are often held in executive session, contrary to what many feel is essential to a democracy.

After all hearings have been completed and the members of the subcommittee have had an opportunity to examine the transcript of the hearings in its entirety (many members are not present for all the hearings), the subcommittee holds an executive session on the bill to discuss the issues and ultimately to vote on the bill. At this time they may amend the bill in any way they desire, they may report the bill to the parent committee with a favorable or an unfavorable recommendation, or they may recommend that the parent committee table the bill. The recommendation of the subcommittee will be considered by the parent committee but is not binding in any way.

The standing committees meet regularly each week to hear the reports of the subcommittees. Again full discussion ensues on a particular bill, amendments may be made, and a vote is finally taken either to report the bill to the House (with or without amendments) or to table the bill in the committee. An unfavorable report is seldom made. A bill may be forced out of a committee by the use of a discharge petition, but this is rare and is politically dangerous.

This procedure may all seem simple. In essence it is. In actuality, the power of the chairman of the committee and of the subcommittee is great; either of them is often able to block action on a bill simply by not scheduling a time for the committee to hear the bill. It is difficult to challenge the chairman's authority to "pigeon-hole" a bill.

3. *Reporting the Bill.* If the committee votes favorably on the bill, the following occurs:

(a) A member voting favorably on the bill is assigned to write a majority report spelling out the broad purposes of the bill and explaining why the committee voted favorably on it. All existing laws which will be changed by the bill must be indicated and any laws repealed must be specified.

(b) Provision must be made for a minority report to be filed. This report explains in detail the reasons for opposition to the bill and lays the groundwork for the opposition when the bill comes up for full debate.

(c) The report is assigned a report number and is sent to the Government Printing Office for overnight printing. The bill is also printed in official form showing committee amendments in italics and indicating any deletions from the original by stricken-through type.

(d) The report number is printed on the bill and both are assigned a calendar number.[5]

4. *Assignment to a Calendar.* A public bill—a bill which is general in nature and does not seek relief for an individual or small group—will generally be referred to the Union Calendar or to the House Calendar. The Union Calendar gets its name from the provision in the House rules that there shall be a calendar ". . . of the Committee of the Whole House on the State of the Union. . . ." Bills which raise revenues or which directly or indirectly appropriate money for activities of a general character are placed on this calendar. Most public bills are in this category.

The rules also provide for a House Calendar on which are placed all public bills which do not raise revenue and which do not directly or indirectly appropriate money. Those public bills which are not first placed on the Union Calendar are put on the House Calendar.

Public bills which are not controversial may be transferred to

[5] See page 176 for an example of a bill as reported from a House committee.

the Consent Calendar to expedite the legislative process. Any bill which is favorably reported by a committee and placed on the Union or the House Calendar may be transferred to the Consent Calendar by any member of the House. On the first and third Mondays of each month the bills on the Consent Calendar are called up. If no one objects and if there is no request that the bill be "passed over," it is considered as passed by unanimous consent without debate. If there is an objection by one or two members, the bill is carried over to the next date for considering the Consent Calendar. An objection by three or more members forces the bill off the Consent Calendar and returns it to the Union or the House Calendar.

The Representative who places the bill on the Consent Calendar is expected to clear it with the major opposition; if he does his job well, the whole process is streamlined. Each party selects three members whose job it is to study bills on the Consent Calendar in order that something does not "slip through"; they serve as "official objectors" if the bill falls into categories which have been established by the parties in the House.

All private bills, those which are not general in character but are directed at one person or a very few people, are placed on the Private Calendar and may be called up on the first and third Tuesdays of each month. An objection by two or more members recommits the bill to the committee which reported it originally. The parties also maintain "official objectors" to police the Private Calendar.

5. *Getting Consideration of the Bill.* Placement on the House or Union Calendar does not guarantee that a bill will ever be considered by the House. Many bills die on the Calendar each session. Bills are of varying importance; priority must be given to some measures, and too much time should not be spent in debate over less important but controversial matters. Establishing these priorities is a complex problem with no easy solution. The Committee on Rules does most of this work.

The Committee on Rules became a standing committee in 1880;

led by Thomas Brackett "Czar" Reed, the powers of the committee were subsequently expanded. In 1890 it was given the power to report at any time, in 1893 it received the privilege of sitting while the House was in session, and in 1895 the Rules Committee began to take control of the decision on what bills were to be released for Floor vote. At present, the Rules Committee has almost complete control over the agenda of the House through the issuance of special "rules" which determine when and for how long a bill will be debated. Usually the chairman of the committee which has favorably reported the bill, the sponsor of the bill, and several supporters appear before the Committee on Rules and ask that a special "Rule" be issued. If their request is granted, the bill will be brought up before the House for consideration and action.

If they get an unfavorable response or if a bill has been held up by one of the standing committees for over thirty days, a motion to discharge and a discharge petition are in order. These are rarely used, and only then when there is strong demand in the face of a recalcitrant chairman or members of the committee. The threat of a discharge motion sometimes is sufficient to get action if the chairman feels that there is a pretty good possibility that the petition and the motion will receive the required majority.

Under special conditions, with two-thirds of the members voting affirmatively, a quorum being present, the rules can be suspended and a bill or resolution considered. This is difficult except for urgent matters and is used infrequently.

Calendar Wednesday is another device for calling a bill off the Calendar. On Wednesday of each week the Speaker calls each standing committee in alphabetical order; each committee can call up any bill previously reported by it which is pending on the Union or House Calendar. A maximum of two hours equally divided between the two sides is allowed for debate on the measure. Obviously not many bills can be heard under these conditions.

As mentioned above, the Committee on Rules has the right to call up bills and resolutions at any time. These are regarded as "privileged" questions; that is, they take priority over other considerations in the order of business. The Committee on Appropriations on general appropriations bills and the Committee on Ways and Means on bills raising revenues also have the power to declare their actions privileged. The member in charge of a bill in one of these categories may call it up at almost any time for immediate consideration.

6. *The Ordeal of Consideration.* According to the rules of the House all bills and resolutions on the Union Calendar must, after a special resolution or "rule" from the Committee on Rules, be heard by the Committee of the Whole, as it is usually called. Under this procedure the House is able to act with much more ease since the normal rules for Floor debate are abridged. A quorum for the Committee of the Whole is composed of 100 members rather than 218, a majority of the membership.

The Speaker appoints a chairman and steps down from his chair. The bill is debated and the "second reading of the bill" section by section begins. Amendments are made, with each member who wishes to speak on an amendment limited to five minutes. Each is voted on by the Committee of the Whole. Some of these amendments are aimed at clarifying or strengthening the bill. Many of them are designed to "cripple" the bill. Because the yea-and-nay vote which identifies each member's position is not used in the Committee of the Whole, it is impossible to have an accurate record of the votes of members.

The Committee of the Whole either rejects the bill, which kills it, or votes to report favorably to the House, which then reconvenes and receives the report of the Committee. The House members proceed to act on the bill. There may be further debate on the bill if permitted by the original Rule.

Measures on the House, Private, and Consent Calendars do not have to go through the Committee of the Whole and are considered by the House directly, with the ground rules established by the Committee on Rules.

After debate the Speaker asks the question, "Shall the bill be engrossed and read a third time?" If the House votes affirmatively the bill is read, usually by title only, and the House adopts the measure. (If the vote is negative, the bill is dead.)[6]

The bill is ordered to be engrossed, i.e., it is printed in the form in which it was finally passed with all amendments. The Clerk of the House signs the measure and, with all due dignity and ceremony, the bill is delivered to the Senate where it must begin the second part of the journey toward becoming a law.

LEGISLATION AND THE SENATE

1. *Assignment to Committee.* Upon receipt of the bill from the House, the President of the Senate assigns it to the proper standing committee for its consideration. As already mentioned in the discussion on the House, this is often a complex and crucial decision.

2. *Action in the Committee.* Consideration by subcommittee and then full committee in the Senate follows much the same pattern as in the House. There are detailed hearings by the subcommittee and eventually its members report to the parent committee, favorably or unfavorably, on the original act or on the act as they have amended it. In the consideration by the whole committee, the bill may again be amended; it is then reported to the Senate favorably or tabled by the committee (unfavorable reports are rare). If a committee fails to act on a measure in a reasonable time or if the measure has been tabled, any Senator may move to discharge the committee from further consideration. When a bill is reported out (or when the committee is discharged from further consideration of the bill), it is placed on the Calendar of Bills under the standing rules. As in the House, the report includes the hearings, the majority report, and any minority reports made.

[6] Congress (for some reasons and many excuses) has not seen fit to install voting machines in either house. A yea-and-nay vote is taken in the House only on the request of one-fifth of the members present. An accurate record is possible, therefore, in only a few instances. Under present conditions such a vote is time-consuming and is taken only when enough Congressmen feel they should "stand up and be counted."

3. *Action on the Floor*. Action in the Senate is more formal in many ways than in the House—and yet the Senate is even more of a "club" in its atmosphere.

There is only one calendar in the Senate, the Calendar of General Bills. When a report is to be made of committee action on a bill, the Senator responsible formally states that he is reporting the bill. If the bill is noncontroversial, he may ask for unanimous consent to hear the bill at once. If there is no objection, Floor action begins immediately. There may be amendments at this time, and after a brief though unlimited debate, final action will be taken. If there is an objection, the bill must lie over one day and then, like all the others which have merely been reported, it takes its place on the Calendar.

By their own rules, the Senate must consider the Calendar every legislative day, though they may side-step this in one of two ways: by recessing rather than adjourning at the end of the day, or by seeking and gaining unanimous consent to dispense with the call of the Calendar. The majority policy committee of the Senate determines which items shall be considered and the times at which they will be considered, except for the relatively few bills of a noncontroversial nature which are taken up in their order on the Calendar or which have been called up by a Senator. The Majority Leader usually moves that the Senate consider a bill at a given time. This motion is subject to debate. If the issue is of particular importance or of strong emotional content to one or a few of the Senators, a filibuster may develop in an attempt to prevent the bill from even being considered by the Senate, or to wrangle concessions from the majority when the bill does come up. If no one objects to the Majority Leader's motion, the bill is scheduled for Senate consideration. For this reason, the parties (or factions within them) have "objectors" who are supposed to examine all Calendar items and be prepared to object to these motions. An example of a maneuver used to forestall these objectors' activities came in the spring of 1960, when the Majority Leader moved that the Senate consider a bill dealing with a military base.

There were no objections. When the bill came up for consideration the leader announced that it was subject to amendment and, amid the cries of "foul" from certain southern Senators, a substantial civil rights amendment was moved. While this did not forestall an "extended debate" on civil rights, it did get the issue on the Floor for debate and resulted in eventual passage of a civil rights bill in a modified form.

Under the present rules it is very difficult to close the debate in the Senate if the Senators desire to have an extended debate (filibuster). Debate may be closed only if sixteen Senators sign a motion to limit the debate and that motion (which is not debatable) is passed by two-thirds (sixty-seven) of the Senate. Attempts to amend this rule have been unsuccessful.

Debate continues on amendments submitted, and finally on the bill as amended. If it passes at this stage, the bill comes up for the third reading, usually by title only, and the final vote is taken. As is the case with the House, there are no mechanical voting devices and many of the votes are not recorded. A simple majority is necessary for final passage.

The original engrossed bill and the Senate's amendments, if any, are then returned to the House with a report on the Senate action. If there have been any Senate amendments the report contains a formal request that the House accept them.

JOINT ACTION BY THE TWO HOUSES

If there have been no Senate amendments, the bill is enrolled and awaits action by the President. If, however, it is passed in an amended form it must be returned to the house in which it originated, in this case the House of Representatives, for further action. If the Senate amendments are minor or noncontroversial they may be adopted by the House by unanimous consent. If there is objection, however, the amended act becomes privileged and may be called for immediate consideration by a simple motion. When, after debate, the amendments to which there have been objections are passed by a simple majority, the bill is completed and awaits presidential action.

However, when the amendments are extensive or strong and cannot be accepted by the House, a conference is requested with the Senate and "managers" are appointed by the Speaker to represent the House in the conference. There are usually three members, but sometimes more, in the House delegation to the conference. By custom, the House delegation is bipartisan or is made up of members of the same party who are on opposite sides of the issue. If the Senate agrees to the conference—this is almost automatic—a similar group is appointed by the President of the Senate to attempt to satisfy the desires of both houses. The conferees are permitted to negotiate only over those areas (perhaps substantial, perhaps minor) in which the two houses have disagreed. If one house or the other gives in completely or (more likely) a compromise is worked out, the committee produces a report in duplicate which must be signed by a majority of the "managers" from each house. There is no minority report.

The house which agreed to the requested conference, in this instance the Senate, acts first on the bill as reported out of the conference committee. The report may not be amended; it must be adopted or rejected in its entirety. If the act is approved, it is transmitted to the other house where similar rules apply.

If the conference committee cannot agree on some of the amendments or cannot reach a satisfactory compromise within the committee, a report of this failure is filed; in our example, the Senate receives the report first. By a simple majority vote it may recede from any or all of its amendments. If it clings to some of them, a record of the action with or without a request for another conference is forwarded to the House of Representatives. If the House accepts the bill as it has now been modified, it is ready for Presidential action. If it cannot agree to any remaining amendments, the conference process begins again and continues until agreement is reached—or until a complete impasse is reached.

Once a bill has been agreed to in identical form by both houses, it must be meticulously written down in its final form. All amendments must truly reflect the action of the houses. All punctuation must be exactly as adopted by the houses (even if the enrolling clerks believe it is grammatically wrong!). The enrolled bill is printed on parchment paper, signed by the Clerk of the House, approved for accuracy by the Subcommittee on Enrolled Bills of the Committee on House Administration, and sent to the Speaker for his signature. It goes to the Senate to be checked for accuracy, and to be signed by the President of the Senate. The bill is then presented to the President for his action.

PRESIDENTIAL ACTION

Article I, Section VII, of the Constitution provides that

Every bill which shall have passed the House of Representatives and the Senate shall, before it becomes a law, be presented to the President of the United States; if he approves he shall sign it, but if not he shall return it, with his objections, to the house in which it shall have originated, who shall enter the objections at large on their journal and proceed to reconsider it. If after such reconsideration two-thirds of that house shall agree to pass the bill, it shall be sent, together with the objections, to the other house, by which it shall likewise be reconsidered, and if approved by two-thirds of that house it shall become a law. . . . Any bill not returned by the President within ten days (Sundays excepted) after it shall have been presented to him, the same shall be a law, in like manner as if he had signed it, unless the Congress by their adjournment prevent its return, in which case it shall not be a law.

When a bill is presented to the President it is circulated to all departments and agencies directly concerned with the subject matter for advice on the various provisions. As the Constitution dictates, the President must take action in a short time, in one of these several ways:

1. He may sign the bill and it becomes law.

2. He may refuse to sign the bill and return it, with his objections, to the house in which the bill originated. Thus we say he has

vetoed the bill. Technically he has only suspended action for the time being, hence his action is referred to as a suspension veto.[7]

3. He may not sign the bill and yet not return it with his objections to its house of origin within the Constitutional period of ten days (Sundays excepted). If Congress is still in session, the bill becomes a law without the President's approval. The Constitution prevents the President from holding up legislation to which he objects but which Congress might desire strongly enough to override an actual veto.

4. If the bill is presented to him during the last nine days (Sundays excepted) of a session, the President need not sign the bill or use his suspension veto. He merely fails to take action or, as the saying goes, "he puts it in his pocket," and the bill dies. Hence the term "pocket veto." Such presidential action is not subject to being overridden by Congress. This is a protection against the mass of legislation which Congress may grind out in the closing days of a term without considering wisely, in their hurry to escape from the confines of a muggy Washington summer and to return to political fence-mending in their own districts.

If the President signs the bill it is customary that he send a message to the originating house informing the members of his action. A report of his signing is printed in the *Congressional Record*.

If, however, the President uses his suspension veto, he returns the bill to the originating house with his objections—he considers the act unwise, he feels that the act is contrary to the Constitution, he has opposed such acts in his campaign and the people have elected him on these statements, etc. Veto messages vary greatly in length.

A vetoed bill has a privileged standing; a motion to consider it is always in order. The Constitution requires that this be a yea-and-nay vote and that the names of those voting for and against be printed in the *Journal*. If fewer than two-thirds of a quorum of the originating house vote to override the President's veto, the

[7] See page 166 for an example of a presidential veto message.

other house is so informed and the bill is dead. If two-thirds of a quorum vote "yea," the bill (with the President's objections and a report of the action in the originating house) is sent to the other house. If they also agree by a two-thirds vote to override the veto, the bill becomes law over the President's veto.

After approval by the President or passage by the Congress over his veto, the law is sent to the Administrator of Public Services where it is duly published.

Simple, is it not? It may sound so, but a mechanical survey does not take into consideration the vitally important human element in lawmaking. That human element—as it expresses itself in leadership, in the seniority system of committee assignment, in the work of pressure groups, in the status of members, and in the ability to speak on the Floor at the right times, for example—makes the machine work in ways not dreamed of by the uninitiated.

APPENDIX

SELECTED BIBLIOGRAPHY

There are many works, both scholarly and popular, to assist the reader in his attempt to understand Congress. For further reading on the work of Congress in general and on the House of Representatives in particular, the following are recommended:

STEPHEN K. BAILEY, *Congress Makes a Law,* Columbia University Press, New York, 1950, is a very readable book which traces the path of a single controversial bill through Congress.

STEPHEN K. BAILEY and HOWARD D. SAMUEL, *Congress at Work,* Henry Holt, New York, 1953, is a series of studies of selected congressmen at work.

DONALD C. BLAISDEL, *American Democracy Under Pressure,* Ronald Press, New York, 1957. This developed from an earlier TNEC report which the author wrote; it does a good job of examining pressure activities.

JAMES M. BURNS, *Congress on Trial,* Harper, New York, 1949, criticizes Congress through the study of three important bills which the author felt illustrated the need for stronger Presidential leadership of Congress.

ALLEN DRURY, *Advise and Consent,* Doubleday, Garden City, 1959, is a novel by an experienced Washington correspondent. Despite its length, it gives an interesting, if sometimes superficial, picture of political forces at play in the confirmation of a Presidential appointment.

GEORGE B. GALLOWAY, *The Legislative Process in Congress,* Thomas Y. Crowell, New York, 1953, gives a good picture of the mechanics of Congress at work. It is largely descriptive, a good reference work.

ERNEST S. GRIFFITH, *Congress in its Contemporary Role,* 3d ed., New York University Press, New York, 1961, is available in paperback and is a successful attempt at presenting the mechanics of Congress.

BERTRAM M. GROSS, *The Legislative Struggle,* McGraw-Hill, New York, 1953, is a particularly valuable study of intergroup conflict in Congress.

PENDLETON HERRING, *Group Representation Before Congress,* Johns Hopkins University Press, Baltimore, 1929, is still a very valuable examination of the role of pressure groups in Congress.

DONALD R. MATTHEWS, *U. S. Senators and Their World,* University of North Carolina Press, Chapel Hill, 1960, is the best analytical study of the Senate. It is strongly recommended.

GILBERT STEINER, *The Congressional Conference Committee,* University of Illinois Press, Urbana, 1951, is an interesting study of a particular type of committee which gives an insight into some of the other workings of Congress.

JULIUS TURNER, *Party and Constituency,* Johns Hopkins University Press, Baltimore, 1951, presents another view on party regularity in Congress. It is valuable reading.

DAVID B. TRUMAN, *The Congressional Party,* John Wiley, New York, 1959, is an interesting analysis of the party structure in Congress.

DOCUMENTS

On pages 165 to 169 are reproduced five documents, some in part and some complete, which represent the diversity of the business of Congress. On the remaining pages of this section are reproduced in part the documents which record the congressional history of one bill which created the Arms Control Agency.

87TH CONGRESS
1ST SESSION

H. CON. RES. 296

IN THE HOUSE OF REPRESENTATIVES

MAY 8, 1961

Mr. MERROW submitted the following resolution; which was considered and agreed to

CONCURRENT RESOLUTION

1   *Resolved by the House of Representatives (the Senate*

2   *concurring),* That the Congress hereby commends Com-

3   mander Alan B. Shepard, Junior, United States Navy, of

4   Derry, New Hampshire, for his outstanding achievement and

5   the courage and skill displayed by him in his flight into space

6   on May 5, 1961, in the Mercury capsule known as Free-

7   dom 7.

WILLIAM JOSEPH VINCENT

MESSAGE

FROM

THE PRESIDENT OF THE UNITED STATES

TRANSMITTING

WITHOUT APPROVAL THE BILL (H.R. 3498) FOR THE RELIEF OF
WILLIAM JOSEPH VINCENT

MAY 29, 1961.—Referred to the Committee on the Judiciary and ordered to be
printed

To the House of Representatives:

I am returning herewith, without my approval, H.R. 3498, for the relief of William Joseph Vincent.

This bill proposes that this veteran be relieved of an obligation to repay non-service-connected pension payments which he received while ineligible. Payments depended upon his annual compensation and he misinformed the Veterans' Administration of the amount of this compensation.

The facts were easily obtainable by the veteran. The overpayment and consequent repayment obligation resulting from the misinformation are, of course, unfortunate, but the fault was clearly that of the claimant and not of the Government.

Approval of this bill would adversely affect administration of the program of veteran benefits and seriously discriminate against thousands of other similarly situated veterans. It is important that all veterans and their dependents be similarly treated and that we preserve the integrity and impartiality which are essential. This we cannot do if we grant special privilege and favored treatment to one or a few or allow profit from misrepresentation.

JOHN F. KENNEDY.

THE WHITE HOUSE, *May 26, 1961.*

87TH CONGRESS
1ST SESSION

H. RES. 127

IN THE HOUSE OF REPRESENTATIVES

JANUARY 24, 1961

Mr. TRIMBLE submitted the following resolution; which was referred to the House Calendar and ordered to be printed

JANUARY 31, 1961

Considered and agreed to

RESOLUTION

1   *Resolved,* That during the Eighty-seventh Congress the

2 Committee on Rules shall be composed of fifteen members.

S. 604

IN THE SENATE OF THE UNITED STATES

JANUARY 26, 1961

Mr. LONG of Missouri (for himself, Mr. CASE of South Dakota, Mr. CHAVEZ, Mr. CLARK, Mr. ENGLE, Mr. GRUENING, Mr. HUMPHREY, Mr. JAVITS, Mr. KEATING, Mr. LONG of Hawaii, Mr. MORSE, Mr. MOSS, Mr. PROXMIRE, and Mrs. SMITH of Maine) introduced the following bill; which was read twice and referred to the Committee on Rules and Administration

A BILL

To revise the Federal election laws, to prevent corrupt practices in Federal elections, and for other purposes.

1 *Be it enacted by the Senate and House of Representa-*

2 *tives of the United States of America in Congress assembled,*

3 That this Act may be cited as the "Federal Elections Act of

4 1961".

87TH CONGRESS
1ST SESSION

H. J. RES. 505

IN THE HOUSE OF REPRESENTATIVES

JULY 26, 1961

Mr. VINSON introduced the following joint resolution; which was referred to the Committee on Armed Services

---

JOINT RESOLUTION

To authorize the President to order units and members in the Ready Reserve to active duty for not more than twelve months, and for other purposes.

1   *Resolved by the Senate and House of Representatives*

2   *of the United States of America in Congress assembled,*

3   That, notwithstanding any other provision of law, until

4   July 1, 1962, the President may, without the consent of

5   the persons concerned, order any unit, and any member not

6   assigned to a unit organized to serve as a unit, in the Ready

7   Reserve of an armed force to active duty for not more than

8   twelve consecutive months. However, not more than two

9   hundred and fifty thousand members of the Ready Reserve

THE PASSAGE OF THE ARMS CONTROL AGENCY ACT

Congress moves in "fits and starts." At times it moves with astonishing rapidity and at other times with frustrating slowness. Congress often takes several years to act on an idea. Sometimes this inaction springs from an apparent lack of interest on the part of the President as well as the Congress. This seems to have been true of the idea for an Arms Control Agency, which was finally created in the closing days of the congressional session in September, 1961.

Several bills had been introduced in previous years but languished in the legislative labyrinth. In 1961, President Kennedy took office. The Arms Control Agency seemed to him needed and worthy of urging Congress to act. On June 29, 1961, President Kennedy wrote the following letter to Speaker Rayburn.

THE WHITE HOUSE
WASHINGTON

June 29, 1961

Dear Mr. Speaker:

I am transmitting herewith, for consideration by the Congress, a draft of legislation to carry out the recommendation contained in my May twenty-fifth Message, for the establishment of a strengthened and enlarged disarmament agency to make an intensified effort to develop acceptable political and technical alternatives to the present arms race.

Today, ability of man to master his environment threatens to outpace his ability to control himself. The world is more and more interdependent, and the people of the earth can now look beyond this planet to a new age of discovery, but they have not yet been able to banish the primitive threat of war. The ingenuity that has made the weapons of war vastly more destructive should be applied to the development of a system of control of these weapons.

But peace cannot be brought about by concentrating solely on measures to control and eliminate weapons. It must also encompass measures to sustain and strengthen international institutions and the rule of law. A disarmament program must take into account the national security; our foreign policy; the relationships of this country to international peace-keeping agencies, including the United Nations; and our domestic economic and other policies. It should drive toward the creation of a peaceful world society in which disarmament, except for the forces needed to apply international sanctions, is the accepted condition of international life.

For the past five months, Mr. John J. McCloy, my advisor on disarmament matters, has been conducting, at my request, an extensive study of the governmental effort and organization necessary to give effect to our national purpose in this field. He has had available to him the results of searching studies by individual members and committees of the Congress, the agencies of Government principally concerned, national and international organizations and eminent private individuals. During the course of his study, Mr. McCloy has consulted closely with Secretary Rusk, Secretary McNamara, Chairman Seaborg and other high officials. All of these studies and consultations have inescapably pointed to the conclusion that a new effort, considerably larger than our present effort, in terms of size, range of skills and authority will be necessary. This can best be accomplished by the creation of a new United States agency.

Following Mr. McCloy's recommendations, I am therefore proposing that a new United States Disarmament Agency for World Peace and Security be established. Enactment of the proposed legislation will permit this agency to deal broadly with the whole range of disarmament matters, including research, policies, and programs.

The importance and broad scope of disarmament matters require continuing Presidential attention. The complex inter-relationships between disarmament activities, foreign affairs, and national security also require that close working-level coordination and cooperation be established between the new agency and the Departments of State and Defense, the Atomic Energy Commission, and other agencies.

The proposed legislation provides that the Director of the new agency function under the direction of the President and the Secretary of State. This arrangement will permit coordination of disarmament matters within the purview of the various agencies; it will give special recognition to the need for intermeshing disarmament policies and programs with the broad conduct of foreign affairs; and it will provide a focal point at the highest level of Government for the consideration of disarmament matters.

In the light of these unique relationships the Director, as the principal advisor to the President in the disarmament field, will have direct access to him but will, of course, notify the Secretary of State as to the occasion and substance of the advice he offers. In addition, the Director will report to the Secretary of State, without going through intermediate authority, and he will act as the agent of the Secretary of State with authority, under his direction, to act in his name. Also, I intend that he participate in all meetings of the National Security Council having to do with disarmament.

I am enclosing a letter from Mr. McCloy describing the legislation in more detail.

Sincerely yours,

Honorable Sam Rayburn
Speaker of the
House of Representatives
Washington, D. C.

Only a member of Congress may introduce a bill—and more than one may be introduced on the same topic simultaneously in both houses. In this instance, on the day the President wrote his letter seventy-one identical or similar bills were introduced. One of them was introduced by Thomas E. Morgan, Chairman of the Committee on Foreign Affairs. The bill was referred to Morgan's committee for consideration.

87TH CONGRESS
1ST SESSION

H. R. 7936

IN THE HOUSE OF REPRESENTATIVES

JUNE 29, 1961

Mr. MORGAN introduced the following bill; which was referred to the Committee on Foreign Affairs

A BILL

To establish a United States Disarmament Agency for World Peace and Security.

1   *Be it enacted by the Senate and House of Representa-*

2   *tives of the United States of America in Congress assembled,*

3   TITLE I—SHORT TITLE, PURPOSE, AND

4   DEFINITIONS

5   SHORT TITLE

6   SECTION 1. This Act may be cited as the "Disarmament

7   Act for World Peace and Security".

8   PURPOSE

9   SEC. 2. An ultimate goal of the United States is a world

10 which is free from the scourge of war and the dangers and

11 burdens of armaments; in which the use of force has been

Some 180 pages of hearings were held in late August and early September.

TO ESTABLISH A UNITED STATES ARMS CONTROL AGENCY

HEARINGS

BEFORE THE

COMMITTEE ON FOREIGN AFFAIRS
HOUSE OF REPRESENTATIVES

EIGHTY-SEVENTH CONGRESS

FIRST SESSION

ON

H.R. 7936 and H.R. 9118

AUGUST 24, 25, 28, AND SEPTEMBER 7, 1961

Printed for the use of the Committee on Foreign Affairs

U.S. GOVERNMENT PRINTING OFFICE
WASHINGTON : 1961

These hearings, staff work, and the give and take of the committee process led Chairman Morgan to submit a "clean" bill on September 11. This bill incorporated those changes necessary to make the bill acceptable to the committee.

87TH CONGRESS
1ST SESSION

H. R. 9118

IN THE HOUSE OF REPRESENTATIVES

SEPTEMBER 11, 1961

Mr. MORGAN introduced the following bill; which was referred to the Committee on Foreign Affairs

A BILL

To establish a United States Arms Control Agency.

1   *Be it enacted by the Senate and House of Representa-*

2   *tives of the United States of America in Congress assembled,*

3   TITLE I—SHORT TITLE, PURPOSE, AND

4   DEFINITIONS

5   SHORT TITLE

6   SECTION 1. This Act may be cited as the "Arms Con-

7   trol Act".

8   PURPOSE

9   SEC. 2. An ultimate goal of the United States is a world

10   which is free from the scourge of war and the dangers and

11   burdens of armaments; in which the use of force has been

87TH CONGRESS	HOUSE OF REPRESENTATIVES	REPORT
1st Session		No. 1165

ESTABLISHING A U.S. ARMS CONTROL AGENCY

SEPTEMBER 12, 1961.—Committed to the Committee of the Whole House on the State of the Union and ordered to be printed

Mr. MORGAN, from the Committee on Foreign Affairs, submitted the following

REPORT

[To accompany H.R. 9118]

The Committee on Foreign Affairs, to whom was referred the bill (H.R. 9118) to establish a U.S. Arms Control Agency, having considered the same, report favorably thereon without amendment and recommend that the bill do pass.

NEED FOR LEGISLATION

This legislation, providing for the establishment of a U.S. Arms Control Agency, does not reflect any intention that the United States give a higher priority to disarmament than to defense, or that we intend to disarm in the face of a military threat.

The United States believes that the day will come when it will be possible to assure our own security and world peace with only a fraction of the manpower and the resources now devoted to military functions. It has been and will continue to be our policy to hasten the realization of this objective.

At the same time we do not intend to disarm when such a course will endanger our security.

The horrors of nuclear warfare, combined with the existence of the United Nations to focus world opinion on arms control and disarmament and to facilitate negotiation, assure that the United States will be increasingly concerned with problems of the limitation, reduction, and control of armaments.

These problems are complex and highly technical, involving considerations of scientific development, foreign policy, and military strategy. We can best assure that our security will not be endangered if we are able to bring to bear on these problems all of the pertinent knowledge and skill which we possess.

Union Calendar No. 501

87TH CONGRESS
1ST SESSION

H. R. 9118

[Report No. 1165]

IN THE HOUSE OF REPRESENTATIVES

SEPTEMBER 11, 1961

Mr. MORGAN introduced the following bill; which was referred to the Committee on Foreign Affairs

SEPTEMBER 12, 1961

Committed to the Committee of the Whole House on the State of the Union and ordered to be printed

---

A BILL

To establish a United States Arms Control Agency.

1 *Be it enacted by the Senate and House of Representa-*

2 *tives of the United States of America in Congress assembled,*

3   TITLE I—SHORT TITLE, PURPOSE, AND

4   DEFINITIONS

5   SHORT TITLE

6   SECTION 1. This Act may be cited as the "Arms Con-

7 trol Act".

8   PURPOSE

9   SEC. 2. An ultimate goal of the United States is a world

10 which is free from the scourge of war and the dangers and

11 burdens of armaments; in which the use of force has been

« 176 »

The Committee on Rules granted a rule (H. Res. 462) to bring the bill up for consideration by the House; the resolution established the limits for debate on the bill. On September 19, Congressman Thomas P. O'Neill, Jr., of the Committee on Rules moved H. Res. 462; following limited debate on the resolution it was agreed to by voice vote.

Congressional Record, September 19, 1961

TO ESTABLISH A U.S. ARMS CONTROL AGENCY

Mr. O'NEILL. Mr. Speaker, by direction of the Committee on Rules, I call up the resolution (H. Res. 462) and ask for its immediate consideration.

The Clerk read the resolution as follows:

Resolved, That upon the adoption of this resolution it shall be in order to move that the House resolve itself into the Committee of the Whole House on the State of the Union for the consideration of the bill (H.R. 9118) to establish a United States Arms Control Agency, and all points of order against said bill are hereby waived. After general debate, which shall be confined to the bill and continue not to exceed two hours, to be equally divided and controlled by the chairman and ranking minority member of the Committee on Foreign Affairs, the bill shall be read for amendment under the five-minute rule. At the conclusion of the consideration of the bill for amendment, the Committee shall rise and report the bill to the House with such amendments as may have been adopted, and the previous question shall be considered as ordered on the bill and amendments thereto to final passage without intervening motion except one motion to recommit.

ESTABLISHING A U.S. ARMS CONTROL AGENCY

Mr. MORGAN. Mr. Speaker, I move that the House resolve itself into the Committee of the Whole House on the State of the Union for the consideration of the bill (H.R. 9118) to establish a U.S. Arms Control Agency.

The motion was agreed to.

Accordingly the House resolved itself into the Committee of the Whole House on the State of the Union for the consideration of the bill H.R. 9118, with the gentleman from Tennessee [Mr. DAVIS] in the chair.

The Clerk read the title of the bill.

By unanimous consent, the first reading of the bill was dispensed with.

The CHAIRMAN. Under the rule, the gentleman from Pennsylvania [Mr. MORGAN] will be recognized for 1 hour and the gentlewoman from Ohio [Mrs. BOLTON] will be recognized for 1 hour.

The Chair recognizes the gentleman from Pennsylvania [Mr. MORGAN].

(Mr. MORGAN asked and was given permission to revise and extend his remarks.)

Mr. MORGAN. Mr. Chairman, I yield myself 10 minutes.

Mr. Chairman, I rise in support of the bill H.R. 9118.

Mr. Chairman, there is more misunderstanding concerning what this bill is all about than any piece of legislation which I can recall. A good many people apparently have the idea that the President wants to set up a special agency to deal with matters relating to disarmament to work against the Defense Department and the Atomic Energy Commission. They seem to think the proposed Agency is supposed to favor disarmament as opposed to defense. I note that there are various groups with pacifist leanings who favor the bill because they think it is antimilitary, and various veterans organizations oppose the bill apparently for the same reason.

The fact of the matter is that there is nothing antimilitary about the bill. The new Agency will make our defenses stronger rather than weaker.

The committee received testimony strongly supporting the bill from the Honorable Roswell L. Gilpatric, Deputy Secretary of Defense in the present administration—Secretary McNamara was unavailable at the time—and from the Honorable Thomas S. Gates, Jr., who was Secretary of Defense during the Eisenhower administration. Gen. Lyman L. Lemnitzer, Chairman of the Joint Chiefs of Staff, also testified in favor of the bill.

After constituting themselves as the Committee of the Whole House on the State of the Union, H. R. 9118 was read for amendment under the five-minute rule. The committee agreed to the bill. It then "rose," reconstituted itself as the House, and moved to the final roll call vote on the bill which passed by a vote of 216 to 54 with 91 not voting.

Congressional Record, September 19, 1961

Mr. MORGAN. If the gentleman will yield, we accept the amendment.

The CHAIRMAN. Without objection, the amendment is agreed to.

There was no objection.

The CHAIRMAN. If there are no further amendments, under the rule, the Committee will rise.

Accordingly the Committee rose, and the Speaker pro tempore [Mr. McCORMACK] having resumed the Chair, Mr. DAVIS of Tennessee, Chairman of the Committee of the Whole House on the State of the Union reported that that Committee having had under consideration the bill (H.R. 9118) to establish a U.S. Arms Control Agency, pursuant to House Resolution 462, he reported the bill back to the House with sundry amendments adopted in Committee of the Whole.

The SPEAKER pro tempore. Under the rule, the previous question is ordered.

Is a separate vote demanded on any amendment? If not, the Chair will put them en gros.

The SPEAKER pro tempore. The question is on the amendments.

The amendments were agreed to.

The SPEAKER pro tempore. The question is on the engrossment and third reading of the bill.

The bill was ordered to be engrossed and read a third time and was read the third time.

The SPEAKER pro tempore. The question is on the passage of the bill.

Mr. JOHANSEN. Mr. Speaker, I offer a motion to recommit.

The SPEAKER pro tempore. Is the gentleman opposed to the bill?

Mr. JOHANSEN. I am, Mr. Speaker.

The SPEAKER pro tempore. The Clerk will report the motion to recommit.

The Clerk read as follows:

Mr. JOHANSEN moves to recommit the bill, H.R. 9118, to the Committee on Foreign Affairs.

The SPEAKER pro tempore. The question is on the motion to recommit.

The motion was rejected.

The SPEAKER pro tempore. The question is on the passage of the bill.

Mr. GROSS. Mr. Speaker, I ask for the yeas and nays.

The yeas and nays were ordered.

The question was taken; and there were—yeas 290, nays 54, not voting 91, as follows:

[Roll No. 216]

YEAS—290

Abbitt	Conte	Green, Pa.
Abernethy	Cook	Griffin
Adair	Corbett	Griffiths
Addabbo	Corman	Gubser
Addonizio	Cramer	Hagan, Ga.
Albert	Cunningham	Hagen, Calif.
Andersen,	Curtin	Halleck
Minn.	Curtis, Mass.	Halpern
Andrews	Curtis, Mo.	Hansen
Ashley	Daddario	Harding
Aspinall	Daniels	Hardy
Avery	Davis, John W.	Harris
Bailey	Davis, Tenn.	Harvey, Ind.
Baker	Dawson	Hays
Baldwin	Delaney	Healey
Baring	Dent	Hechler
Barrett	Denton	Hemphill
Barry	Diggs	Henderson
Bass, N.H.	Dingell	Herlong
Bates	Donohue	Holifield
Becker	Downing	Holland
Beckworth	Doyle	Horan
Belcher	Dulski	Hosmer
Bennett, Fla.	Durno	Huddleston
Betts	Dwyer	Hull
Blatnik	Edmondson	Ikard, Tex.
Blitch	Elliott	Inouye
Boland	Ellsworth	Jarman
Bolling	Everett	Jennings
Bolton	Evins	Joelson
Bonner	Fallon	Johnson, Calif.
Bow	Fascell	Johnson, Md.
Boykin	Feighan	Jonas
Brademas	Fenton	Jones, Ala.
Bray	Finnegan	Judd
Breeding	Fino	Karsten
Brewster	Fisher	Kastenmeier
Bromwell	Flood	Kee
Brooks	Flynt	Keith
Broomfield	Fogarty	Kelly
Brown	Forrester	Keogh
Broyhill	Fountain	Kilday
Burke, Ky.	Frelinghuysen	Kilgore
Burke, Mass.	Friedel	King, Calif.
Byrne, Pa.	Fulton	King, Utah
Cahill	Gallagher	Kitchin
Cannon	Garland	Kluczynski
Cederberg	Garmatz	Knox
Chamberlain	Gary	Kornegay
Chelf	Giaimo	Kowalski
Chenoweth	Glenn	Kunkel
Clancy	Goodell	Kyl
Clark	Granahan	Landrum
Coad	Grant	Lane
Cohelan	Gray	Langen
Collier	Green, Oreg.	Lankford

Latta	Murray	Schwengel
Lennon	Natcher	Scott
Lesinski	Nelsen	Scranton
Libonati	Nix	Seely-Brown
Lindsay	Norbald	Selden
McCormack	Nygaard	Shipley
McDowell	O'Brien, Ill.	Shriver
McFall	O'Hara, Ill.	Sibal
McIntire	O'Hara, Mich.	Slack
McMillan	Olsen	Smith, Miss.
McSween	O'Neill	Smith, Va.
Macdonald	Ostertag	Springer
Mack	Patman	Stafford
Madden	Perkins	Staggers
Magnuson	Philbin	Stephens
Mahon	Pike	Stratton
Mailliard	Poage	Stubblefield
Marshall	Poff	Sullivan
Martin, Mass.	Price	Taylor
Mathias	Pucinski	Thompson, N.J.
Matthews	Quie	Thompson, Tex.
May	Randall	Thomson, Wis.
Merrow	Reece	Thornberry
Miller, Clem	Reifel	Tollefson
Miller,	Rhodes, Pa.	Trimble
George P.	Riehlman	Tuck
Milliken	Rivers, Alaska	Tupper
Mills	Roberts	Ullman
Minshall	Robison	Vanik
Moeller	Rodino	Van Zandt
Monagan	Rogers, Colo.	Wallhauser
Moore	Rogers, Fla.	Walter
Moorehead,	Rogers, Tex.	Watts
Ohio	Rooney	Whalley
Moorhead, Pa.	Rostenkowski	Whitener
Morgan	Roush	Wickersham
Morris	Ryan	Widnall
Morrison	St. Germain	Wright
Morse	Santangelo	Yates
Mosher	Schneck	Young
Moss	Schneebeli	Zablocki
Murphy	Schweiker	

NAYS—54

Alford	Gavin	Rhodes, Ariz.
Alger	Goodling	Riley
Anderson, Ill.	Gross	Rivers, S.C.
Ashbrook	Haley	Roudebush
Ashmore	Harrison, Wyo.	Rousselot

Beermann	Harvey, Mich.	Rutherford
Bennett, Mich	Hiestand	Saylor
Bruce	Hoffman, Ill.	Scherer
Burleson	Hoffman, Mich.	Smith, Calif.
Casey	Jensen	Taber
Davis,	Johansen	Teague, Tex.
James C.	King, N.Y.	Udall, Morris K.
Derounian	Lipscomb	Utt
Devine	McVey	Van Pelt
Dole	Meader	Williams
Dominick	O'Konski	Wilson, Ind.
Dorn	Passman	Winstead
Findley	Pillion	
Gathings	Ray	

NOT VOTING—91

Alexander	Hoeven	Rabaut
Anfuso	Holtzman	Rains
Arends	Ichord, Mo.	Reuss
Auchincloss	Johnson, Wis.	Roosevelt
Ayres	Jones, Mo.	St. George
Bass, Tenn.	Karth	Saund
Battin	Kearns	Schadeberg
Bell	Kilburn	Shelley
Berry	Kirwan	Sheppard
Boggs	Laird	Short
Buckley	Loser	Sikes
Byrnes, Wis.	McCulloch	Siler
Carey	McDonough	Sisk
Celler	MacGregor	Smith, Iowa
Chiperfield	Martin, Nebr.	Spence
Church	Mason	Steed
Colmer	Michel	Teague, Calif.
Cooley	Miller, N.Y.	Thomas
Dague	Montoya	Thompson, La.
Derwinski	Moulder	Toll
Dooley	Multer	Vinson
Dowdy	Norrell	Weaver
Farbstein	O'Brien, N.Y.	Weis
Ford	Osmers	Westland
Frazier	Pelly	Wharton
Gilbert	Peterson	Whitten
Hall	Pfost	Willis
Harrison, Va.	Pilcher	Wilson, Calif.
Harsha	Pirnie	Younger
Hébert	Powell	Zelenko

So the bill was passed.

87TH CONGRESS
1ST SESSION

S. 2180

IN THE SENATE OF THE UNITED STATES

JUNE 29, 1961

Mr. HUMPHREY (for himself, Mr. SPARKMAN, Mr. WILEY, Mr. COOPER, Mr. HART, Mr. CLARK, Mr. ANDERSON, Mr. RANDOLPH, and Mr. McGEE) introduced the following bill; which was read twice and referred to the Committee on Government Operations

---

A BILL

To establish a United States Disarmament Agency for World Peace and Security.

1   *Be it enacted by the Senate and House of Representa-*

2 *tives of the United States of America in Congress assembled,*

3   TITLE I—SHORT TITLE, PURPOSE, AND

4   DEFINITIONS

5   SHORT TITLE

6   SECTION 1. This Act may be cited as the "Disarmament

7 Act for World Peace and Security".

8   PURPOSE

9   SEC. 2. An ultimate goal of the United States is a world

10 which is free from the scourge of war and the dangers and

S. 2180 was referred originally to the Committee on Government Operations. On August 3 this committee was discharged from consideration and the bill was then referred to the Committee on Foreign Relations which in mid-August held hearings on it; a 352-page transcript of the hearings was printed.

DISARMAMENT AGENCY

HEARINGS

BEFORE THE

COMMITTEE ON FOREIGN RELATIONS

UNITED STATES SENATE

EIGHTY-SEVENTH CONGRESS

FIRST SESSION

ON

S. 2180

A BILL TO ESTABLISH A UNITED STATES DISARMAMENT AGENCY FOR WORLD PEACE AND SECURITY

———

AUGUST 14, 15, AND 16, 1961

———

Printed for the use of the Committee on Foreign Relations

U.S. GOVERNMENT PRINTING OFFICE

WASHINGTON : 1961

Calendar No. 864

| 87th Congress *1st Session* | SENATE | Report No. 882 |

UNITED STATES DISARMAMENT AGENCY FOR WORLD PEACE AND SECURITY

September 6, 1961.—Ordered to be printed

Mr. Humphrey, from the Committee on Foreign Relations, submitted the following

REPORT

[To accompany S. 2180]

The Committee on Foreign Relations, having had under consideration the bill (S. 2180) to establish a U.S. Disarmament Agency for World Peace and Security, reports the same with amendments and recommends that, as amended, it be passed by the Senate.

MAIN PURPOSE

S. 2180, as amended by the Committee on Foreign Relations, will establish within the Department of State a new governmental agency, the U.S. Disarmament Agency. This Agency will be under the direction of the Under Secretary of State for Disarmament, hereinafter referred to as the Director, who

> shall serve as the principal adviser to the Secretary of State and the President on disarmament matters.

The Agency is to be responsible, under the direction of the Secretary of State, for the acquisition of a fund of practical and theoretical knowledge about disarmament and is directed to conduct research in that field, to engage public or private institutions or persons for such studies, and to coordinate work in this field now being undertaken by other Government agencies in accordance with procedures to be established by the President. Not to exceed $10 million is authorized to be appropriated for the purposes of the act and to remain available until expended.

BACKGROUND

Since the end of World War II, there have been a large number of international conferences and meetings attended by both the United States and the Soviet Union at which disarmament matters have been discussed. The organization of the executive branch for this activity

87TH CONGRESS
1ST SESSION

S. 2180

[Report No. 882]

IN THE SENATE OF THE UNITED STATES

JUNE 29, 1961

Mr. HUMPHREY (for himself, Mr. SPARKMAN, Mr. WILEY, Mr. COOPER, Mr. HART, Mr. CLARK, Mr. ANDERSON, Mr. RANDOLPH, Mr. McGEE, Mr. CASE of New Jersey, Mrs. NEUBERGER, Mr. JAVITS, Mr. PELL, Mr. PASTORE, and Mr. PROXMIRE) introduced the following bill; which was read twice and referred to the Committee on Government Operations

AUGUST 3, 1961

The Committee on Government Operations discharged, and referred to the Committee on Foreign Relations

SEPTEMBER 6, 1961

Reported by Mr. HUMPHREY, with amendments

[Omit the part struck through and insert the part printed in italic]

A BILL

To establish a United States Disarmament Agency for World Peace and Security.

1   *Be it enacted by the Senate and House of Representa-*

2   *tives of the United States of America in Congress assembled,*

3   TITLE I—SHORT TITLE, PURPOSE, AND

4   DEFINITIONS

5   SHORT TITLE

6   SECTION 1. This Act may be cited as the "Disarmament

7   Act for World Peace and Security".

When the bill was brought to the floor, debate lasted only part of the day, September 8; the bill passed 73 to 14 and was forwarded to the House of Representatives for consideration.

Congressional Record, September 8, 1961

The PRESIDING OFFICER. The bill having been read the third time, the question is, Shall it pass? The yeas and nays have been ordered, and the clerk will call the roll.

The legislative clerk called the roll.

Mr. SMATHERS. On this vote I have a pair with the senior Senator from Illinois [Mr. DOUGLAS]. Were he present and voting he would vote "yea." Were I at liberty to vote, I would vote "nay." I therefore withold my vote.

Mr. HUMPHREY. I announce that the Senator from Illinois [Mr. DOUGLAS], the Senator from Arkansas [Mr. FULBRIGHT], the Senator from Arizona [Mr. HAYDEN], the Senator from Wyoming [Mr. McGEE] and the Senator from Massachusetts [Mr. SMITH] are absent on official business.

I also announce that the Senator from New Mexico [Mr. CHAVEZ] and the Senator from New Mexico [Mr. ANDERSON] are absent because of illness.

I further announce that, if present and voting, the Senator from New Mexico [Mr. ANDERSON], the Senator from New Mexico [Mr. CHAVEZ], the Senator from Arkansas [Mr. FULBRIGHT], the Senator from Arizona [Mr. HAYDEN], the Senator from Wyoming [Mr. McGEE] and the Senator from Massachusetts [Mr. SMITH] would each vote "yea."

Mr. KUCHEL. I announce that the Senator from Vermont [Mr. AIKEN] is absent on official business.

The Senator from Utah [Mr. BENNETT] and the Senator from North Dakota [Mr. YOUNG] are necessarily absent.

The Senator from New Hampshire [Mr. BRIDGES] and the Senator from Kansas [Mr. CARLSON] are absent because of illness.

If present and voting, the Senator from Utah [Mr. BENNETT] and the Senator from Kansas [Mr. CARLSON] would each vote "yea."

The result was announced—yeas 73, nays 14, as follows:

[No. 192]

YEAS—73

Allott	Gruening	Miller
Bartlett	Hart	Monroney
Beall	Hartke	Morse
Bible	Hickenlooper	Morton
Boggs	Hickey	Moss
Burdick	Hill	Muskie
Bush	Holland	Neuberger
Butler	Humphrey	Pastore
Byrd, W. Va.	Jackson	Pell
Cannon	Javits	Prouty
Capehart	Johnston	Proxmire
Carroll	Jordan	Randolph
Case, N.J.	Keating	Robertson
Case, S. Dak.	Kefauver	Saltonstall
Church	Kerr	Scott
Clark	Kuchel	Smith, Maine
Cooper	Lausche	Sparkman
Cotton	Long, Mo.	Symington
Dirksen	Long, Hawaii	Wiley
Dodd	Long, La.	Williams, N.J.
Dworshak	Magnuson	Williams, Del.
Engle	Mansfield	Yarborough
Ervin	McCarthy	Young, Ohio
Fong	McNamara	
Gore	Metcalf	

NAYS—14

Byrd, Va.	Hruska	Stennis
Curtis	McClellan	Talmadge
Eastland	Mundt	Thurmond
Ellender	Russell	Tower
Goldwater	Schoeppel	

NOT VOTING—13

Aiken	Chavez	Smathers
Anderson	Douglas	Smith, Mass.
Bennett	Fulbright	Young, N. Dak.
Bridges	Hayden	
Carlson	McGee	

So the bill (S. 2180) was passed, as follows:

Be it enacted by the Senate and House of Representatives of the United States of America in Congress assembled,

87TH CONGRESS
1ST SESSION

S. 2180

IN THE HOUSE OF REPRESENTATIVES

SEPTEMBER 11, 1961
Referred to the Committee on Foreign Affairs

AN ACT

To establish a United States Arms Control and Disarmament Agency for World Peace and Security.

1   *Be it enacted by the Senate and House of Representa-*

2   *tives of the United States of America in Congress. assembled,*

3   TITLE I—SHORT TITLE, PURPOSE, AND

4   DEFINITIONS

5   SHORT TITLE

6   SECTION 1. This Act may be cited as the "Arms Con-

7   trol and Disarmament Act for World Peace and Security".

The two houses had passed bills which differed in title and in wording yet which were quite similar. For the agency to become a reality, both houses had to pass the same identical bill and have it approved by the President. The Senate made the first effort toward a common bill on September 20, when Senator Fulbright moved that H. R. 9118, which had been forwarded to the Senate for action, be amended to be identical with the wording of S. 2180. H. R. 9118, as amended, then passed the Senate by a voice vote without debate. Mr. Fulbright then moved that the Senate insist upon its amendment, and request a conference with the House to work out the differences between the two houses on H. R. 9118.

Congressional Record, September 20, 1961

U.S. ARMS CONTROL AGENCY

Mr. FULBRIGHT. Mr. President, I move that the Senate proceed to the consideration of House bill 9118, to establish a U.S. Arms Control Agency.

The motion was agreed to; and the Senate proceeded to consider the bill (H.R. 9118) to establish a U.S. Arms Control Agency, which was read twice by its title.

Mr. FULBRIGHT. Mr. President, this bill was only recently passed by the House of Representatives.

I move that all after the enacting clause of the bill be stricken out, and that there be inserted in lieu thereof the text of Senate bill 2180, to establish a U.S. Disarmament Agency for World Peace and Security.

The PRESIDING OFFICER. The question is on agreeing to the motion of the Senator from Arkansas.

The motion was agreed to.

The PRESIDING OFFICER. The question now is on the engrossment of the amendment and the third reading of the bill.

The amendment was ordered to be engrossed and the bill to be read a third time.

The bill (H.R. 9118) was read the third time and passed.

The PRESIDING OFFICER. Without objection, the title to H.R. 9118 will be amended to read "to establish a U.S. Disarmament Agency for World Peace and Security."

Mr. FULBRIGHT. Mr. President, I move that the Senate insist upon its amendment, request a conference thereon with the House of Representatives, and that the Chair appoint the conferees on the part of the Senate.

The motion was agreed to; and the Presiding Officer appointed Mr. FULBRIGHT, Mr. SPARKMAN, Mr. HUMPHREY, Mr. SYMINGTON, Mr. WILEY, and Mr. HICKENLOOPER the conferees on the part of the Senate.

| 87TH CONGRESS
1st Session | HOUSE OF REPRESENTATIVES | REPORT
No. 1263 |

ARMS CONTROL AND DISARMAMENT ACT

SEPTEMBER 23 (legislative day, SEPTEMBER 22), 1961.—Ordered to be printed

Mr. MORGAN, from the committee of conference, submitted the following

CONFERENCE REPORT

[To accompany H.R. 9118]

The committee of conference on the disagreeing votes of the two Houses on the amendment of the Senate to the bill (H.R. 9118) to establish a United States Arms Control Agency, having met, after full and free conference, have agreed to recommend and do recommend to their respective Houses as follows:

That the House recede from its disagreement to the amendment of the Senate to the text of the bill and agree to the same with an amendment as follows:

In lieu of the matter proposed to be inserted by the Senate amendment insert the following:

TITLE I—SHORT TITLE, PURPOSE, AND DEFINITIONS

SHORT TITLE

SECTION 1. This Act may be cited as the "Arms Control and Disarmament Act".

PURPOSE

SEC. 2. An ultimate goal of the United States is a world which is free from the scourge of war and the dangers and burdens of armaments; in which the use of force has been subordinated to the rule of law; and in which international adjustments to a changing world are achieved peacefully. It is the purpose of this Act to provide impetus toward this goal by creating a new agency of peace to deal with the problem of reduction and control of armaments looking toward ultimate world disarmament.

Arms control and disarmament policy, being an important aspect of foreign policy, must be consistent with national security policy as a whole. The formulation and implementation of United States arms control and

The same day the conference committee reported, Congressman Morgan brought the bill to the floor of the House where, after brief debate, it was passed 252 to 50.

Congressional Record, September 23, 1961

Mr. MORGAN. Mr. Speaker, I move the previous question on the conference report.

The previous question was ordered.

The SPEAKER pro tempore. The question is on the conference report.

The question was taken, and the Speaker pro tempore announced that the ayes appeared to have it.

Mr. GROSS. Mr. Speaker, I object to the vote on the ground that a quorum is not present, and make the point of order that a quorum is not present.

The SPEAKER pro tempore. Evidently a quorum is not present.

The Doorkeeper will close the doors, the Sergeant at Arms will notify absent Members, and the Clerk will call the roll.

The question was taken; and there were—yeas 252, nays 50, not voting 133, as follows:

[Roll No. 226]

YEAS—252

Addabbo	Cahill	Forrester
Addonizio	Cannon	Fountain
Albert	Chamberlain	Frelinghuysen
Alexander	Cheif	Friedel
Andersen,	Chenoweth	Fulton
Minn.	Church	Gallagher
Andrews	Clancy	Garmatz
Arends	Clark	Gary
Ashley	Coad	Giaimo
Aspinall	Cohelan	Gilbert
Avery	Conte	Granahan
Ayres	Cook	Grant
Bailey	Cramer	Gray
Baker	Curtin	Green, Oreg.
Baldwin	Curtis, Mass.	Green, Pa.
Baring	Daddario	Gubser
Barrett	Dague	Hagan, Ga.
Barry	Davis, John W.	Hagen, Calif.
Bates	Dawson	Halleck
Beckworth	De:aney	Harding
Belcher	Denton	Hardy
Bennett, Fla.	Derwinski	Harris
Betts	Dingell	Harrison, Wyo.
Blatnik	Donohue	Harsha
Boland	Downing	Healy
Bolling	Doyle	Hechler
Bolton	Dulski	Hemphill
Bonner	Durno	Henderson
Bow	Dwyer	Holland
Boykin	Edmondson	Hosmer
Brademas	Elliott	Huddleston
Bray	Everett	Ichord, Mo.
Breeding	Fallon	Ikard, Tex.
Brewster	Farbstein	Inouye
Bromwell	Fenton	Jarman
Brooks	Finnegan	Jennings
Broomfield	Fisher	Joelson
Brown	Flood	Johnson, Calif.
Broyhill	Flynt	Johnson, Md.
Burke, Mass.	Fogarty	Jonas
Byrne, Pa.	Ford	Jones, Ala.

Judd	Montoya	Schweiker
Karsten	Moore	Schwengel
Kastenmeier	Moorehead,	Scott
Kearns	Ohio	Scranton
Kee	Moorehead, Pa.	Seely-Brown
Kilgore	Morgan	Selden
King, Calif.	Morris	Shipley
King, Utah	Morse	Shriver
Kirwan	Mosher	Sibal
Kitchin	Murphy	Sikes
Kluczynski	Murray	S.sk
Knox	Natcher	Slack
Kornegay	Nix	Smith, Iowa
Kowalski	Nygaard	Smith, Miss.
Kunkel	O'Brien, Ill.	Spence
Lane	O'Brien, N.Y.	Springer
Langen	O'Hara, Ill.	Staggers
Lankford	O'Hara, Mich.	Steed
Latta	Olsen	Stephens
Lennon	O'Neill	Stratton
Lesinski	Ostertag	Stubblefield
McCormack	Passman	Taylor
McCulloch	Patman	Thomas
McDowell	Perkins	Thompson, N.J.
McFall	Peterson	Thompson, Tex.
McMillan	Pfost	Thomson, Wis.
Mack	Philbin	Thornberry
Madden	Pike	Toll
Magnuson	Poff	Trimble
Mahon	Price	Udall, Morris K.
Mailliard	Pucinski	Ullman
Marshall	Randall	Vanik
Mathias	Reece	Van Zandt
Matthews	Rivers, Alaska	Walter
May	Roberts	Watts
Merrow	Robison	Weis
Miller, Clem.	Rogers, Colo.	Whalley
Miller,	Rogers, Fla.	Whitener
George P.	Rogers, Tex.	Whitten
Milliken	Rooney	W.ckersham
Mills	Roush	W.dnall
Minshall	Ryan	W.llis
Moelier	St. Germain	Yates
Monagan	Schneebeli	Zablocki

NAYS—50

Abbitt	Dowdy	Ray
Anderson, Ill.	Gathings	Rhodes, Ariz.
Ashbrook	Gavin	Rivers, S.C.
Ashmore	Goodling	Roudebush
Auchincloss	Gross	Rousselot
Battin	Haley	Rutherford
Beermann	Hoffman, Ill.	Saylor
Bruce	Jensen	Schadeberg
Burleson	Johansen	Scherer
Casey	King, N.Y.	Sheppard
Cunningham	Laird	Taber
Davis,	Lipscomb	Teague, Tex.
James C.	McVey	Tuck
Derouinan-	Mason	Utt
Dole	Meader	Wilson, Calif.
Dominick	Norrell	W.lson, Ind.
Dorn	O'Konski	Winstead

NOT VOTING—133

Abernethy	Frazier	Macdonald
Adair	Garland	MacGregor
Alford	Glenn	Martin, Mass.
Alger	Goodell	Martin, Nebr.
Anfuso	Griffin	Michel
Bass, N.H.	Griffiths	Miller, N.Y.
Bass, Tenn.	Hall	Morrison

Becker	Halpern	Moss	Davis, Tenn.	Keogh	Rodino
Bell	Hansen	Moulder	Dent	Kilburn	Roosevelt
Bennett, Mich.	Harrison, Va.	Multer	Devine	Kilday	Rostenkowski
Berry	Harvey, Ind.	Nelsen	Diggs	Kyl	St. George
Blitch	Harvey, Mich.	Norblad	Dooley	Landrum	Santangelo
Boggs	Hays	Osmers	Ellsworth	Libonati	Saund
Buckley	Hébert	Pelly	Evins	Lindsay	Schenck
Burke, Ky.	Herlong	Pilcher	Fascell	Loser	Shelley
Byrnes, Wis.	Hiestand	Pillion	Feighan	McDonough	Short
Carey	Hoeven	Pirnie	Findley	McIntire	Siler
Cederberg	Hoffman, Mich.	Poage	Fino	McSween	Smith, Calif.
Celler	Holifield	Powell	Smith, Va.	Tupper	Wharton
Chiperfield	Holtzman	Quie	Stafford	Van Pelt	Williams
Collier	Horan	Rabaut	Sullivan	Vinson	Wright
Colmer	Hull	Rains	Teague, Calif.	Wallhauser	Young
Cooley	Johnson, Wis.	Reifel	Thompson, La.	Weaver	Younger
Corbett	Jones, Mo.	Reuss	Tollefson	Westland	Zelenko
Corman	Karth	Rhodes, Pa.			
Curtis, Mo.	Keith	Riehlman			
Daniels	Kelly	Riley			

So the conference report was agreed to.

The Senate, also on September 23, discussed H. R. 9118 as it was reported by the conference committee and agreed to the changes by a voice vote.

Congressional Record, September 23, 1961

Mr. SPARKMAN. Mr. President, I wish to add a word to what has been said. The Senator from Louisiana could not be present at this time. He is greatly interested in this matter. He is concerned that perhaps the wording we have added weakened the provision as he offered it in the Foreign Relations Committee and as it was agreed to on the part of the Senate. Personally, I did not feel it has the same effect the Senator from Louisiana felt it had. The big difference between the House and the Senate was how much of the knowledge or information obtained by a private individual in connection with inventions or patents that may have been developed while he was employed by the Government had to be divulged to the other side. I felt the language we adopted provided full and fair consideration. However, the Senator from Louisiana does not feel that way. I have assured him, as has the Senator from Minnesota, as has the chairman of the Foreign Relations Committee, Mr. FUL-BRIGHT, who, unfortunately, had to leave before we took up the conference report, that if the language proves to weaken the provision, we shall certainly join with the Senator from Louisiana at the first opportunity in an effort to get the language restored in such a way that it will do the job intended.

We did not retain the Agency completely within the Department of State, as the Senate had it; nor did we retain it as a completely independent agency, as the House had it. We did give it autonomy and a high degree of independence. We gave the Director the right to report directly to the President and made him the principal adviser to the President on arms control and disarmament matters; but, likewise, placed the Agency under the direction and supervision of the Secretary of State, because of its implications in foreign policy.

I believe we worked out a very good solution, and I hope the Senate will approve the conference report.

The PRESIDING OFFICER. The question is on agreeing to the conference report.

The report was agreed to.

The act was printed in its final form, signed by the presiding officers of the House and Senate, and presented to the President for his approval. The act was approved by the President on September 26, 1961 at New York City.

H. R. 9118—9

United States Code; entertainment and official courtesies to the extent authorized by appropriation; expenditures for training and study; expenditures in connection with participation in international conferences for the purposes of this Act; and expenses in connection with travel of personnel outside the United States, including transportation expenses of dependents, household goods, and personal effects, and expenses authorized by the Foreign Service Act of 1946, as amended, not otherwise provided for.

APPROPRIATION

Sec. 49. (a) There are hereby authorized to be appropriated not to exceed $10,000,000 to remain available until expended, to carry out the purposes of this Act.

(b) Funds appropriated pursuant to this section may be allocated or transferred to any agency for carrying out the purposes of this Act. Such funds shall be available for obligation and expenditure in accordance with authority granted in this Act, or under authority governing the activities of the agencies to which such funds are allocated or transferred.

REPORT TO CONGRESS

Sec. 50. The Director shall submit to the President, for transmittal to the Congress, not later than January 31 of each year, a report concerning activities of the Agency.

Speaker pro tempore of the House of Representatives.

Vice President of the United States and President of the Senate.

Approved —
12:45 P.M. SEP 26 1961
New York City — New York,

John F. Kennedy

(Carlyle Hotel

A report of the President's remarks on signing the act was released to the press,

IMMEDIATE RELEASE, SEPTEMBER 26, 1961

OFFICE OF THE WHITE HOUSE PRESS SECRETARY

THE WHITE HOUSE
(NEW YORK, N. Y.)

REMARKS OF THE PRESIDENT
ON SIGNING H.R.9118, AN ACT TO ESTABLISH THE
UNITED STATES ARMS CONTROL AND DISARMAMENT AGENCY
(AT THE CARLYLE HOTEL IN NEW YORK CITY)

With the signing of H.R. 9118, there is created the United States Arms Control and Disarmament Agency. This Act symbolizes the importance the United States places on arms control and disarmament in its foreign policy.

The creation for the first time by Act of Congress of a special organization to deal with arms control and disarmament matters emphasizes the high priority that attaches to our efforts in this direction.

Our ultimate goal, as the Act points out, is a world free from war and free from the dangers and burdens of armaments in which the use of force is subordinated to the rule of law and in which international adjustments to a changing world are achieved peacefully. It is a complex and difficult task to reconcile through negotiation the many security interests of all nations to achieve disarmament, but the establishment of this Agency will provide new and better tools for this effort.

I am pleased and heartened by the bipartisan support this bill enjoyed in the Congress. The leaders of both political parties gave encouragement and assistance. The new Agency brings renewed hope for agreement and progress in the critical battle for the survival of mankind.

I want to express my thanks to the Members of the Congress, particularly who are here, who were specially interested. I am extremely sorry that Senator Humphrey, who was a particularly vigorous proponent of this legislation for many years in the Senate, is obliged to remain in Washington. And I want to add a special word of thanks to Mr. McCloy, the disarmament adviser, who has given this entire matter his most constant attention.

I want to take this opportunity to announce that the Director of the United States Arms Control and Disarmament Agency set up by this legislation will be Mr. William Foster. He has been a consultant to Mr. McCloy in preparing the American plan which has been submitted to the United Nations General Assembly yesterday, and he and a group have been working for many months, full time, on this most important assignment.

I think that Mr. Salinger can give this afternoon to any members of the press some of the biographical material. Mr. Foster has been a distinguished public servant for many years in the Congress as a most active and leading official in the Marshall Plan. He is a Republican, and I think his appointment indicates the bipartisan, national concern of both parties -- and really, in a sense, all Americans -- for this effort to disarm mankind with adequate safeguards.

So I want to express our appreciation to you, Mr. Foster, for taking on this assignment, and Mr. Salinger perhaps can fill in some of the details. Mr. Foster, as Director of this, has the rank of an Undersecretary of State, and his work will be most closely coordinated with the Secretary of State, with me and the White House and with our representatives in the General Assembly.

END

Public Law 87-297
87th Congress, H. R. 9118
September 26, 1961

An Act

75 STAT. 631.

To establish a United States Arms Control and Disarmament Agency.

*Be it enacted by the Senate and House of Representatives of the
United States of America in Congress assembled,*

TITLE I—SHORT TITLE, PURPOSE, AND DEFINITIONS

SHORT TITLE

SECTION 1. This Act may be cited as the "Arms Control and Disarmament Act".

Arms Control and Disarmament Act.

PURPOSE

SEC. 2. An ultimate goal of the United States is a world which is free from the scourge of war and the dangers and burdens of armaments; in which the use of force has been subordinated to the rule of law; and in which international adjustments to a changing world are achieved peacefully. It is the purpose of this Act to provide impetus toward this goal by creating a new agency of peace to deal with the problem of reduction and control of armaments looking toward ultimate world disarmament.

Arms control and disarmament policy, being an important aspect of foreign policy, must be consistent with national security policy as a whole. The formulation and implementation of United States arms control and disarmament policy in a manner which will promote the national security can best be insured by a central organization charged by statute with primary responsibility for this field. This organization must have such a position within the Government that it can provide the President, the Secretary of State, other officials of the executive branch, and the Congress with recommendations concerning United States arms control and disarmament policy, and can assess the effect of these recommendations upon our foreign policies, our national security policies, and our economy.

This organization must have the capacity to provide the essential scientific, economic, political, military, psychological, and technological information upon which realistic arms control and disarmament policy must be based. It must be able to carry out the following primary functions:

(a) The conduct, support, and coordination of research for arms control and disarmament policy formulation;

(b) The preparation for and management of United States participation in international negotiations in the arms control and disarmament field;

(c) The dissemination and coordination of public information concerning arms control and disarmament; and

(d) The preparation for, operation of, or as appropriate, direction of United States participation in such control systems as may become part of United States arms control and disarmament activities.

DEFINITIONS

SEC. 3. As used in this Act—

(a) The terms "arms control" and "disarmament" mean the identification, verification, inspection, limitation, control, reduction, or elimination, of armed forces and armaments of all kinds under international agreement including the necessary steps taken under such an agreement to establish an effective sytem of inter-

INDEX